MEET THE STARS OF

ANIMORPHS

by Marie Morreale
and Randi Reisfeld

SCHOLASTIC INC.
New York Toronto London Auckland Sydney
Mexico City New Delhi Hong Kong

ISBN 0-439-06165-2

All photos courtesy of Scholastic Entertainment Inc.
Photographer: Steve Wilkie

12 11 10 9 8 7 6 5 4 3 2   9/9 0 1 2 3 4/0

Printed in the U.S.A.

First Scholastic printing, February 1999

INTRODUCTION

The Invasion Has Begun

Once . . . an alien race known as the Andalites bravely battled the Yeerks, a sluglike menace, which spread from planet to planet, conquering species after species like some terrifying disease. For years, the terrible battle waged throughout the galaxy.

Now, five young Earthlings must continue the fight.

That's the theme of *Animorphs,* the coolest, new gotta-see-it TV show, produced by Scholastic Productions. The tele-version of the gripping, megasuccessful Scholastic book series, *Animorphs* revolves around the adventures of those five chosen Earthlings — Jake, Rachel, Marco, Cassie, and Tobias — and their constant battle against . . . well, the end of the world as we know it. And *that's* in addition to having to deal with grades, parents, siblings, clothes, zits, other friends, and the ongoing quest for significant others.

If that's an Everest of stuff to deal with — what*ever*. It's not like they have a choice.

You do. And tuning into *Animorphs* is the coolest one you can make. It's the show everyone at school is already talking about — or will be, soon.

Animorphs is on every Friday night in the Nickel-O-Zone on the Nickelodeon network. And just in case you missed it, the episodes are repeated during Saturday night's SNICK hours.

If you're just catching the Ani-itch and don't know the entire sitch, check it out.

The Backstory

Once . . . Jake, Rachel, Cassie, Marco, and Tobias were pretty normal teens — depending on your definition of normal, that is. They went to school, did their homework, played video games, shopped, hung out. They loved their families unconditionally, respected their teachers, believed in the law, and trusted most other people. That was before.

One fateful day after school, Jake, his cousin Rachel, and their friends Marco and Cassie were hanging out at the video arcade where they were briefly joined by a new kid named Tobias.

Jake had just blasted the competition when, for some bizarre reason, his dog Homer took off out the door. In a flash, Jake, Cassie, Rachel, and Marco dashed after him. The chase led to an abandoned construction site. There they were joined again by Tobias, who often cut through the site on his way home. He happened to get there at the same time. The kids found Homer all right — but at the same time, also witnessed something else.

Tobias saw it first. It was a spaceship, and it was just about to crash. The kids took cover, and watched, mesmerized. After the crash, an actual alien — hooved feet, pointy ears, eye-bearing antennae, glowing green orbs and all — emerged. The alien didn't have a mouth, but that didn't stop him from communicating. It was as if the kids could *hear* his thoughts.

The story he told them, the powers he gave them, and the trust he placed in them, would change their lives forever.

He was Elfangor, a warrior member of a race called Andalites, who lived in another galaxy. For hundreds of years, they'd been battling the evil Yeerks, sluglike creatures whose goal was to transform all living beings of all galaxies into mindless automatons, or Controllers.

The Yeerks were winning the war. They'd worm their way into the ears of all their victims, taking possession of their minds and commanding control of their free will. The Yeerks had already enslaved other planets, crushing all resistance. So far, only the Andalites had managed to escape total annihilation.

The Andalites were able to survive the onslaught because they had a secret "morphing technology." In Elfangor's travels, he'd found out a horrifying secret:

The Yeerks' next destination was planet Earth. That's why he was here, to warn the unsuspecting Earthlings, and to help. But the crash had weakened him, and would soon leave him powerless against the Yeerks who were on his trail.

His last decision before dying: to break Andalite law and empower the five Earthlings he sees — and instinctively trusts — with the secret morphing power. "You must help your world," he beseeched them. "You must protect yourself from the Yeerks."

Elfangor then produced a magical, glowing cube. "Touch the cube," he instructed them. As each one did, he intoned, "The power to change is in your flesh."

The power to change. Jake, Rachel, Cassie, Marco, and Tobias now had the morphing technology: to be able to acquire the DNA of any animal they touch, and morph into the shape of that animal. That, and a mysterious disk, would be their only weapons against the Yeerks.

The whole story sounded crazy. Who'd believe it? The five friends didn't want to. But the longer they stayed at the crash site, the more the terrible truth sank in. Especially after an actual Yeerk appeared and repeated what Elfangor had just said. The horrific creatures really *were* planning to take over the Earth: in fact, they'd already started. To wit: The evil Yeerk then finished Elfangor off.

And then the five were alone: They could trust no one, except each other.

Controllers could be anyone. Their high school principal, teachers, friends — even family — many among them are already Yeerk-infected Controllers. So together, these five teens must outsmart a sinister force unlike any the world has ever known. That's their destiny. From that moment on, the five of them — Jake, Rachel, Cassie, Marco, and Tobias — would be all that stands between life as we know it — and total annihilation. Talk about stress!

The Real Deal

It took five amazing young actors to play the roles of Jake, Tobias, Marco, Rachel, and Cassie — in their human as well as animal forms. All are fresh-faced, megatalented newcomers, and all stand poised to leap from the Nickel-O-Zone to the superstar-zone.

Deborah Forte, executive producer of Animorphs, says, "When we began preproduction of the TV show we knew that the key to the show's success would be finding the right cast. We knew it was critical to find just the right actors who resembled some of the physical characteristics but more importantly, whose personalities were consistent with our characters. We saw hundreds of kids in auditions to find just the right cast. They're all great actors, and they are all great people. And although it's a lot of hard work, they have fun with each other. It's nice to see that they have become friends."

So if you haven't already, memorize these names:

Christopher Ralph (Tobias); Brooke Nevin (Rachel); Shawn Ashmore (Jake); Nadia Nascimento (Cassie); and Boris Cabrera (Marco). For without the magic of the Andalite's gift, high-tech special effects, or sci-fi, they have an amazing power, too. Watch as they morph, right before your eyes, into the hottest new stars on the scene. Here's your exclusive chance to meet them, one by one, up close and personal.

CHAPTER ONE

CHRISTOPHER RALPH
"Tobias is the outsider in the group."

Christopher Ralph plays the brooding, mysterious Tobias. He's the one who didn't know Jake, Rachel, Cassie, and Marco before the incident at the construction site. He's the loner who showed up pretty much the same time Elfangor did with little explanation about his background. Yet in a strange way, he was able to instinctively bond with Jake, Rachel, Cassie, and Marco. The actor who plays him, Christopher Ralph, is every bit as captivating as his complex character — and these days, pretty much *nothing* like him. He used to be, though.

"Tobias is definitely the biggest outsider of the group," Chris says. "He never knew his parents; he was sort of shipped around to aunts and uncles all over the country, so he never had a place to fit in. In that sense, he's sort of a misfit. And even though he really sort of values the friendship of the others, he's

7

still, in many ways, the outsider of the group, very much a loner. He's also a bit of a dreamer."

In real life, there's no mystery about Christopher's background, yet there's a lot about Tobias he can relate to. Growing up, there were times he felt different from the other kids at school, if not a misfit, certainly an outsider.

School Days: Reading, Writing, and — Ridicule?

Christopher Douglas Ralph was born on May 13, 1977, in St. John's, the capital of the Canadian province of Newfoundland, the firstborn son of Douglas and Sandra Ralph. His dad taught junior high school. His mom, a former aide at a Golden Age residence, stayed at home after Chris and his younger brother Gregory were born. "*That,* I guarantee you, was a full-time job!" Chris quips.

As a little kid, Chris was active and happy. "I had a pretty typical childhood," he asserts. He got along with his younger brother, had two or three friends who were always around, and did well in school. "I was pretty keen on it all," he says of elementary school where he excelled in anything to do with reading or English. "I was a voracious reader," Chris says. "At night, after I was supposed to be asleep, I'd slip a flashlight into bed with me and read under the covers. There was this one mystery series, and now I can't remember the name — it wasn't The Hardy Boys — that I was devoted to. Wouldn't miss a single volume.

Aside from those, every once in a while I'd stumble on a big novel."

Even as a little guy, Chris wasn't so "keen" on math. An embarrassing incident involving his first math textbook may be why. "I was in kindergarten, and we were all sitting there with our arithmetic books open. Suddenly, for no reason at all — I mean, I wasn't sick or anything — I threw up, right in the book. It blew my mind! I just looked around and said, 'I don't know how that happened.' Maybe that's why I hated math from that day on. It was like someone tapping me on the shoulder saying, 'You're not gonna go anywhere with math. Forget it, now.'"

In seventh grade, Chris enrolled in I. J. Sampson middle school. There, he got into sports, big time. He played on his school's volleyball and basketball teams. "I was pretty obsessed with basketball," he admits, though he harbored no illusions of ever going pro. "I always played the position of guard, since I was too short to be anything else. I used to stand way outside and take shots, because if I got too near the net, I'd get killed. I wasn't that short, just always a few inches smaller than the other kids who played."

Aside from sports, however, middle school wasn't a good time for Chris. "I didn't like it at all," he candidly confesses. "There was some tension between myself and some of the other kids at school. I mean, I had my couple of friends that I could always depend on, but I didn't care for junior high school a lot. I thought about leaving on many occasions."

With good reason. At different times during his middle-school years, Chris was the kid who got picked on. He says, "For the most part, I avoided fights, but there were a couple of times I was thinking, 'Oh my God, this is the day . . . after school, they're going to get me.'"

Once, "they" did. "There was this guy, he was really trying to make a name for himself. And he figured, a good way to make a name for himself was by picking on me. He just wanted to make my life miserable, so he'd push me around and shove me. I did my best to ignore it. But one day, I guess he just figured 'today's the day I'm gonna make myself known as a tough guy.'

"It happened when I walked down to this store around the corner at lunchtime. There was this huge crowd of kids, and this guy was right in the middle. I was thinking, 'Oh, man, if this isn't for me, I don't know what it's for.' I kept walking and I was about to go in the store when he called me over.

"So I'm standing in front of everybody and they're all looking on. They know what's gonna happen. I'm the only one who's going to be taken by surprise. And then, he came up to me, and decked me — right in the face, right in the chin. He just hauled off and gave me one. And I don't know if it was the adrenaline, or the fear, but I just took it on the chin. And everyone stood there and sort of went, 'ooooh!' He didn't know what to do next. So he said a couple nasty things, and then he realized he wasn't going to get anywhere with me. I just walked away. I just walked back to school. And I think I had [a] little more respect after that."

Chris made sporadic attempts at fitting in and being regarded as cool. Once, his girlfriend told him he'd look better if he bulked up, so he began weight lifting. Big mistake. "I put on fifty pounds really fast," he remembers with a laugh. "I just looked fat. So I stopped and got rid of all that muscle really quickly."

In another middle-school blunder, he recalls, "I cut my hair in this really bad undercut ponytail thing. I shaved it up around the back and the sides and left it long on top. I figured I'd grow it out long and I'd be really stylin'. And it just looked really, really bad!"

Introspective Chris muses, "I've thought about that period in my life quite a bit. And now, the way I see it, in junior high school, I thought I was the only one — but now I realize that every kid thinks he's the only one who isn't cool, who gets picked on. But everyone's getting the same treatment, really. Back then, you don't realize it. You think the whole world is against you, which is complete, just, self-pity, you know? So everyone's going through the same thing. Except for the few people who are, you know, just evil!"

New School, New Challenges

In tenth grade, Chris enrolled in Prince of Wales Collegiate High School. There, things were different, mainly because he was able to get a fresh start. "I went to a different high school [than the other kids in my JHS went to] so I managed to escape in a way."

Yet, he still felt a little like an outsider. "It's like Tobias, because he's a bit of a loner, and seems like he's always got something going on in his head — that makes him weird in high school. And I understand that because I was never one of the popular kids. I mean, it's not like I walked around looking like I was plotting something — I wasn't quite that intense! But there are a number of experiences I had in high school that I can draw from when I'm playing Tobias."

Chris describes himself as the quiet kid who sat in the back, didn't participate more than he had to. He wasn't a troublemaker — though he did get detention once. "Get this," Chris says. "They gave me detention because I skipped a PE class. I had to study for a biology class that I was unprepared for. So I'm in the library and I'm studying for the test, and suddenly the principal's voice comes over the PA system, 'Christopher Ralph, come to the office.' So I come in. . . . They were so disappointed in me. They were like, 'Oh, we can't believe you'd do this!' It's not like they caught me doing something awful! The whole thing was so ridiculous, because these were nice people. The principal was this great guy, a brilliant guy. He genuinely cared about everyone. So, okay, fine I had detention.

"At times during high school, I tried to hang out with the jocks as long as I could — the popular kids. But then I didn't like that anymore — there's just so much aggression you can handle until you say, 'Hey, who you trying to fool? What are you trying to prove?' So I got away from that."

In fact, Chris stopped caring about becoming one of the popular people. "My life was changing, my interests were changing, and I never really bothered to try and get too close to anybody. Again, I had a couple of friends I hung with, and I went to parties, that sort of thing. I just did my own thing, stayed away — I never really liked them."

Although Chris cared a lot about his grades, he wasn't really into his education. "My mind was in other places, I was off someplace else. I wasn't in the classroom when I was in the classroom. Maybe you could say I was a dreamer — but I didn't know it back then."

In spite of that, Chris was a fair student. He was interested in science — sort of. "I thought it was fascinating, but I can't say it was something I loved going to." Math, of course, was still subject non grata. "I hated everything do with it and I despised going to class. I couldn't take it. I'd get headaches thinking about it in the grocery store or something." But his main interests and strengths, continued to be English, literature, and creative writing.

All the way up through his junior year, Chris gave little thought to what he'd do after graduation. Naturally, he was going to college, but he hadn't much of a clue about what he'd major in, let alone what he was going to do with his life. Fleetingly, he'd considered all sorts of possibilities. "At different ages, I had all sorts of ideas. I wanted to be everything from a lawyer, to a police officer, to a writer, absolutely everything under the sun — because I had no idea *what* I wanted to do."

A career as an actor never once entered his mind. "I used to watch a lot of movies," he says, "but I never thought about acting itself, I had no interest in it."

That changed in his senior year of high school. "There was theater arts, this class that was offered, and I decided to take it. I wasn't actually supposed to get in, because I hadn't done the prerequisite courses. But I figured I'd ask. So I went up to the teacher and asked, 'Do you mind if I take this course? There's nothing else I really want to take.' He knew I'd taken creative writing so he figured [I had a real interest in it]. I wasn't just trying to get out of math, or something. So he let me in and I started doing it."

In fact, the teacher, Tolson Carrington, became one of Chris's main influences — and the man to whom the young actor remains most grateful. "From the beginning, even before I ever uttered a line, he had confidence in me. We did a high school drama festival that is an annual event — all the [local] high schools get together at the drama club and produce a show for the festival. There's a student showcase, which my drama teacher was directing. He asked me if I had any ideas. And I had this little thing I'd written up. I'd been carrying it around in my pocket. It was a monologue based on something Bono, from U2, had talked

14

about in a concert. In those days, I was so into U2, I thought Bono was the coolest guy on Earth — the man! Anyway, my teacher read it and said I could perform this. He worked with me on it for three weeks, polishing it. And then he threw me in front of an audience!"

And just like the day that everything changed for Chris's *Animorphs'* character, Tobias, that's when everything came into focus for Christopher Ralph.

Fun With Shakespeare

Okay, well, maybe it wasn't quite that drastic or dramatic. While Chris still insists he really didn't take acting — or anything else — all that seriously, he was intrigued by it. Clearly, he was good at it.

The summer after high school graduation he got together with a few hometown friends and staged some plays. "I did some amateur shows with some friends of mine, which was great, because there are a lot of talented people back home."

And after enrolling at Memorial University in Newfoundland, he dove into the college drama scene. That included a summer Shakespeare festival, which Chris grooved on. "We did *The Taming of the Shrew,* and I had so much fun that I wanted to do it again. There was a lot of Shakespeare going on [in Newfoundland] in the summer."

For the next few years, Chris continued to hone his skills on stage. There was more Shakespeare — Chris acted in *Hamlet* and *Macbeth* — and other classics, including *A Christmas Carol.* Modestly, he reveals, "I usually had principal roles — but I always managed to get a character with a little shadiness or darkness to him. Not exactly villains, but they were all a little bit of a mystery. I really liked that."

Chris had no way of knowing back then, but all that preparation would lead to a new "mystery" character: Tobias.

Morphing Into Tobias

When he was nineteen, Chris moved to Toronto, a big city where there is more opportunity for budding actors. Naturally, he didn't just start getting parts the day he arrived, so he supported himself by doing odd jobs — washing windows, paving driveways, whatever he could get.

At twenty, Chris signed up with an agent, and started the round of tryouts for commercials, TV, and movie parts. He met with lots of rejection — but in a way, that was okay. He'd actually psyched himself for that.

"My agent had forewarned me. He'd said, 'Look, that's what it's all about. Don't get discouraged. Because only one person gets the job, everyone else gets rejected. You have to deal with it.' So I'd planned on [getting into acting] really slowly, I didn't want to put any pressure on myself. Because I knew, if I tried and failed, I wouldn't be able to do it. So my mind-set was,

I just wanted to be there — just be in the game. I wanted to be seen by casting directors and maybe they'd remember me for something else. But it wasn't only about protecting myself. Going to auditions thinking I had nothing to lose, I knew I'd be more relaxed and would do a better job."

Chris's strategy worked — big time. A few months after he began going on auditions, *Animorphs* came along. "Everything happened so quickly — I just feel fortunate to have this role," he marvels.

Hawk Talk

Chris's experiences on and off the *Animorphs* set have been awesome. He bonded with all his costars right away — human *and* animal. Of the former, he says, "We've all hung out together on several occasions after work. We're not always together, but we have good times when we are."

Of the latter, well, Chris admits he had a lot of catching up to do. That's because he really wasn't much of an animal person before *Animorphs* — his family had no pets — but that has all changed.

"The animals are fantastic!" he raves. "We shoot some of our scenes at the Bowmanville Zoo, and all you can see are wild animals running around — lions, elephants, zebras, white tigers. Not that we're ever left alone with the animals, that would be totally against zoo rules. Because the animals are wild, the trainers are always with us — just out of camera range."

Tobias, of course, often morphs into a red-tailed hawk, so that's the creature — or creatures, since *Animorphs* uses three different, identical hawks — Chris has observed most closely. "Doing scenes with the hawk works like this. First, you're just staring at the thing for two hours. You pick up its movements a bit. Not that someone's going to mistake me for a hawk, but I kind of clumsily imitate it." In fact, Chris gained ultimate respect for the hawk. "It's a fantastic creature. I'd never been around one before in my life."

He got to know it a little more intimately than expected. He says, "When they film the hawk, he sort of has this tendency to relieve himself during the take!"

Chris is now so comfortable around animals that he's even adopted one. "I have a cat. It's just a black cat with silver streaks over her eyes. Her name is Pepper. She's fantastic. I never used to like cats before — in fact, I was even against them. I thought they were whiny animals, but I've totally turned around."

On the Home Front

Animorphs is filmed in Toronto, and Chris, along with Pepper, lives in an apartment right in the city. When he's not on-set, or off on location at the zoo, that's where self-described homebody Chris can almost always be found. "I rent a lot of movies," he says. "That way I get to see pretty much everything."

He may be at home at lot, but that doesn't mean he's much of a housekeeper. In other words, the cupboard at this boy's house — and the fridge — are pretty hurtin'. "The thing I reach most often for when I'm hungry is a take-out menu," he admits. Bagels are his usual breakfast, but if he *could* cook, it'd be bacon and eggs. "It makes you feel loved, I find. I like to find a greasy little diner and sit down there."

Going out means going to parties. "I'm not a huge partier, but I go every now and again. And I see my best friend, Scott, who's also moved here from St. John's. We hang out a lot, too."

Since he's been in Toronto, Chris has been so busy, he's been back to St. John's only sporadically. "I miss my friends and family," he concedes. "So when I do go home, I try to squeeze a lot in. When you're visiting only every so often, there're so many people to see, and everyone wants to spend time with you. So it's not relaxing, but it's great. I'd like to get home more often."

Girls: "There's No One Certain Type I Like."

Forget *Animorphs* special effects — Chris has his own very special effect around girls: instant attraction. It's mutual, although candid Chris recalls his first forays into the dating scene as "awkward, awkward, and more awkward!" He claims to not even remember specifics like his first date, first kiss, first real relationship.

What he *does* remember is that "dating" in Newfoundland is not like dating as Americans know it.

19

"It's like this," Chris wryly describes. "You decide to sit next to a girl at a party. And that means you 'like-like' her as opposed to just 'like' her. It sounds sweet, but it's not. It's all these people sitting around, scared to express their feelings!"

Chris has grown a lot since those days. He's been in and out of relationships, and has come to realize that looks don't really mean much, not even at first. "No one can say that there's only one certain type for them because that's not true. You're attracted to someone when there's sort of a spark when you meet — you just feel that you'll go well together. You sense that this is a person you want to hang out with. And that's just as true for when you're meeting a new friend for the first time. You can just tell you're going to get along."

Looking Ahead

Now that Chris has a starring role in a TV series, he's begun to think about looking for other kinds of roles as well. But he's in no hurry.

"I don't set deadlines for myself — like by this age, I want to have achieved this or that. But I do feel fortunate that I'm twenty-one now and I'm not still at home, wondering what I'm going to do with myself. I want to keep going the way I'm going — it sort of blows my mind that I'm even doing this already! This is what you [dream] about. There's nothing else like it. Theater's great, but there's not a lot of money in it. So just that I could be here, in my own apartment, in Toronto, with people paying the rent for me — to do what I'm doing? I would have thought this was beyond my reach. So I have no deadlines. Granted, I'd like to take [acting] as far as it'll go, but however long that takes, we'll have to see."

That said, he admits he'd eventually like to make movies. But he wouldn't settle for any random role. The part would have to be right. "I like sort of layered, interesting, darker roles," he says, "guys that are a little weird, with not just the same typical story that everyone has."

For example? "Edward Scissorhands — that's my dream role. A lot of people don't get that movie, but I do. I really appreciate characters like that one. I'd like to be able to do that one day."

CHAPTER TWO

BROOKE NEVIN
"I can do anything in the world, 'cause I'm Rachel!"

Long blond hair flying in the wind, bright eyes flashing with anticipation and excitement — that's Rachel, the adventurer who's always out-front, ready to try anything, and ready to try it first. Fearless, headstrong, athletic, and smart, Rachel is girl power to the max. It's not by coincidence that her main morph is the lion, the fearless, powerful queen of the jungle.

Brooke Nevin competed against hundreds of hopefuls to play Rachel. No doubt one of the reasons she snagged the part is because she understood the character so well. "Rachel is the bold one," Brooke explains. "She's a little reckless. She'll jump into something feet first without thinking. If there's a challenge, she's the first one to go for it. She has a hot temper sometimes. If someone annoys her, if someone pushes her buttons, she'll get back at that person —

not in mean way, but deliberately. She can get annoyed. She's very pretty. She's very popular in the sense that everyone knows her. She's very in your face, very confident, and fashionable. When I get into my Rachel role, it's like superwoman, girl power! I can do anything in the world, 'cause I'm Rachel."

Off camera, there's a lot of Rachel in sixteen-year-old Brooke — but they're not exactly identical. Brooke explains, "Rachel has much more bravado; she's a lot more daring. I tend to weigh possibilities and consequences a little more than Rachel would. She'd just go ahead and not think twice about doing anything that's on the dangerous side.

"She also tends to hide her emotions a bit more than I do, and put on a brave front. So even if she is scared or emotional, she's not going to let it show. Whereas I find I'm probably a little bit more open with my feelings. You can probably read from my face how I'm feeling, whereas with Rachel she puts on a bit of a poker face. Those would be the main differences," she concludes.

Happy Childhood Memories

Brooke Candice Nevin was born on December 22, 1982, in Toronto, Canada, the city in which she was also raised. A total spotlight-loving ham from the get-go, Brooke used to entertain her parents — mom, Nicky, dad, Bob, and younger sister, Kaleigh, when she was very little. "I've always been into entertaining," she says. "I started in dance class at four years old, and learned tap, jazz, and ballet."

Bubbly Brooke's boundless energy needed other artistic outlets, though, and her supportive parents encouraged her to go for everything. Brooke details, "I was in my school band for three years, playing flute. And my school choir, and also the East York Youth choir, which was like a division in Toronto. Then in middle school, I started in plays. I did school plays and community theater and talent shows."

Brooke cops to having had a terrific childhood. She has always been megaclose with her parents and little sister. She has all sorts of fun memories. "I used to love making original Christmas cards and Mother's Day gifts. I was always into arts and crafts and I'd make big signs and cut out letters. My sister and I would make egg carton flowers for Mom — we'd get really creative and make elaborate cards. We'd spend hours working on one birthday card. And the day would come, and we'd be waiting with anticipation and present it proudly."

Her best adventures, though, took place at her uncle's cabin where the whole extended family would go camping. "It was in northern Quebec, so we had to take a plane there. The first time we went, when I was about twelve, was also my first time on a plane, *and* my first time camping. It was really, really rustic, in the middle of nowhere. We swam in the waterfalls, and swam across the lake; I caught my first fish up there. It was really fun and exciting. We were worried about bears because it was true wilderness out there. We swam in a pool and there were leeches, and my cousin got leeches, and we had to swim really fast, to get away from them. It was wonderful!"

Back then, Brooke was also into reading, big time. *Where the Red Fern Grows* was her favorite book. "I cried at the end because it was so sad," she still remembers.

As she grew, so did her passion to perform. The idea to take her talent to the screen — TV or movies — was purely Brooke's. "I'd been bugging my mom for years to let me get into acting professionally, but we knew it would be a lot of work, so we kept putting it off. Finally, in grade eight, when I was thirteen, I was in a production of the play, *Pirates of Penzance*. I wasn't a main character or anything, but I had really gotten into my role as one of the fifteen daughters. I guess it showed, because after it was over, I got so many compliments on my performance that my mom kind of realized, 'Hey, she *does* have talent.' So that summer, we looked up an agent and I started going on auditions. That was three years ago; that's how long I've been acting professionally."

Of course, acting professionally didn't mean instant fame, fortune, or glamour. "My first role was as an 'extra' — no lines or anything — in a Honeycomb cereal commercial. It *wasn't* fun. There were about fifty other kids and there was so much waiting around. That's when I decided I didn't want to be an 'extra' ever again. I wanted a lead role."

That would take just a few years longer. Before *Animorphs,* Brooke appeared on TV in Canada in *Real Kids — Real Adventures,* and in a *Goosebumps* episode, "A Shocker On Shock Street." She was in a movie called *Short for Nothing,* and most notably, the TV movie that aired on the Showtime cable network called *Running Wild.* To film that, she went to Africa — Brooke's first time outside of Canada. "Being in Africa was the most amazing experience I've ever had," she gushes. "I would love to go back there again."

Last year, when Brooke's agent called to tell her about the tryouts for the part of Rachel in *Animorphs,* she was totally psyched. Not because *she'd* ever heard of the book series — her *friends* definitely had. "So when I said I had this audition, my friends were ecstatic," Brooke explains. Encouraged, Brooke ran out and bought a couple of *Animorphs* books to study for the part.

Her research paid off. It only took Brooke three auditions to nail it. Her friends were almost more excited than she was. "They were like, 'I can't believe it!'" Brooke says. "And then, I went out and got more of the books to read just for pleasure, and I love them. Even if I weren't doing the show, I'd read them. Now, my friends and I, we discuss the books all the time." Brooke doesn't just read the series for fun, though, she uses the books for research. "I've done a lot of character study, making sure that I portray as many character traits as K. A. Applegate displays in her books."

In spite of all that attention to accuracy, Brooke doesn't get ideas or inspiration for Rachel from the *Animorphs* books — but from other characters on TV. "I like *Buffy* [*the Vampire Slayer*] a lot," she admits, "so in certain scenes, I feel that Rachel's going to be a *Buffy* character, strong and determined and really cool and everything."

School Days

When Brooke isn't discussing books with her buds, or being Rachel on *Animorphs*, she's most often in school. An eleventh-grader at Leaside High School, Brooke is a good student who takes a full load of academic courses. "I enjoy most of my subjects," she asserts, adding "in math, we're studying algebra and geometry. I like math, I'm not a whiz or anything, but I like the whole problem solving, the challenge of it, the puzzle you have to figure out. Once you get the answers, it's like, 'Cool — I got it! All right!'"

Science took a little more getting used to, especially the class she was in last year. "It was the first time we'd dissected anything — we had a choice between fish or grasshoppers. I didn't think I'd be able to handle it at first, but then I was okay, and I got interested in the whole process. Of course it was pretty gross when the boys started collecting the eyeballs of the fish! I wouldn't be one to do that."

Brooke's best subject is French. She explains, "Where I go to school, they have a French Immersion program. You can start either in kindergarten or in sixth grade. It means that all your subjects, like math, science, history, art — everything except English and cooking — are taught in French. So, in grade six, I left all my friends in the other class and challenged myself, going into that program. And you go in the first day and the teacher only speaks French. I mean, he speaks a little English, from time to time to help you out, but that's it. So you learn the language quite quickly. Now I'm quite fluent in writing and speaking French. I'm glad I took that program."

Brooke's big on languages. "It just opens your eyes a lot to know another language. It's like a whole new world; I'd like to learn other languages as well." But that's not the only reason for studying French. Her grandparents speak both English and French — "Now, I can understand everything they're saying, especially when they're talking to each other."

The Lion Queen

Even before Brooke landed on *Animorphs*, she was an animal lover. At home, she's got two little dogs, Benji, who is officially her dog, because she saved up to buy him, and Coco, the family canine. But the pitter-patter of pooch paws around the house is nothing compared to the animals Brooke works with on *Animorphs*. Although her character Rachel can morph into everything from a cat to a cockroach, she's most often the lion. "That's definitely Rachel's character," she asserts. Acting "with" a real live beast was amazing. "The first time I saw it, I was so taken aback because I found it so beautiful — it was the most beautiful creature I'd ever seen, especially close up. The eyes, and the whole mane, were especially incredible. I won't say I wasn't scared — I definitely respected it! Especially the time I had to be only one foot away from it, I had to be in the cage with it for that shot. Of course, the trainer was in the cage, too, just out of camera range. But being that close to it — that was amazing!"

More gross than amazing was the time she had to make a hawk jump onto her arm. "To entice it," she disclosed to *Nickelodeon Magazine,* "I had to hold out a chicken leg. Then I watched as it ate the chicken leg right there on my arm, which grossed me out a little bit."

Brooke remembers the first time she actually saw the "finished results" of morphing on screen. "I was so excited," she says, "because the way it looked on screen is exactly the way I imagined it when I read the books." She adds, "Nadia, as Cassie, morphing into the horse, is the best."

Basic Brooke

Off camera and away from the classroom, Brooke's life is pretty normal. She loves bagels — for breakfast, lunch, or a snack anytime — although her favorite food, as a group, is fruit. "My mom has done a good job, drilling into our brain about eating healthy, with veggies and fruit," she explains.

She looks forward to skiing vacations with her family in the Appalachians and never minds baby-sitting her sister. "We get along well," Brooke says.

Rollerblading, biking, and doing sports keep her in shape: Brooke doesn't do any other formal exercise. She's a fan of all different types of music — "I like alternative, classical sometimes, hip-hop, techno even" — she freely admits to being a Spice Girls fan. "They put me in a good mood," she says without apology. So does John Travolta. "With three girls in the house — me, my sister, and Mom, we have a thing for him," she giggles. "We think he's a big sweetheart."

When it comes to fashion, Brooke doesn't exactly have the same passion as Rachel. "I'm a sucker for casual clothes, really," she confesses. "I don't get dressed up too often. I'm a jeans and sweatshirt girl." Unsurprisingly, at the mall, she usually hits The Gap and Roots first. Naturally, she shops with her friends, most of whom she's known since early grade school. "We hang out, we have sleepover parties," Brooke describes.

Between school, *Animorphs*, and being with her friends, Brooke doesn't have a whole lot of time for boys — but that doesn't mean they're not on her mind. She totally knows her type. "I like boys who can make me laugh, who have a good sense of humor, and are sweet, considerate, nice, and cool."

And yet, there's no boyfriend in the picture. In fact, there hasn't been — so far. "Well, only if grade four counts," she says with a laugh. "Otherwise, I haven't. I don't have time, really. I have just enough on my plate, filming and going to school and my days off with my friends. I actually even started dating, but then I kind of stopped. I decided I don't have the time right now. It's not like I can go out, come home late and sleep in the next day. I come home and study, whether it's schoolwork or my script for the next day, and then get up early and go to work. You have to keep your priorities straight, so dating is something that's sort of on hold for now."

The Future

Where does Brooke see herself in the next five years? "If my acting career takes off, then I would seize the opportunity, and make the most of it while I can. I'd like to explore everything. I'd love to do movies. I'm relishing my experience here on *Animorphs* but further down the road, I'm all for movies. I tend to set my goals quite high for myself.

31

My mom always told me, 'The sky's the limit, go for anything, for *everything.*' I'd love to go way up there, for sure!

"But," she adds seriously, "school is a big priority for me — even if I were to become famous, I'd never not go to university, I'd just have to put it on the back burner. But I always see myself finishing my education, no matter how long it takes."

CHAPTER THREE

SHAWN ASHMORE
"Jake is the balance, the center — that's why he's the leader."

"How did *I* get to be the leader?" Jake demands of his friends in one of the first episodes of *Animorphs*. To which Cassie, Rachel, and Marco respond with a shrug, "You just are."

Well, Jake *is* a strong, natural leader-type — but it's not like he ever asked to be in charge of the Animorphs. It just sort of happened that way. So he's a little reluctant about it, and not always comfortable with everyone looking up to him. But he really is mega-responsible, and he'll deal.

Shawn Ashmore will, too — gladly! He's the outgoing, articulate, and awesome young actor who's a perfect fit for Jake's Timberlands. Unsurprisingly, Shawn cops to lots of Jake's character traits.

Here's how the actor describes his TV alter ego: "I see Jake as the responsible one of the group. He kind of balances out everyone else. He's not really outgoing, but he's not really laid back. He's somewhere in the middle. So that makes him the balance, the center. And that's why everyone looks up to him. He was the leader even before they became Animorphs. So even though he comes off as reluctant, I think he likes doing it."

Shawn continues, "I'm kind of like that, too. I'm not exactly a leader, but I've had people tell me that I work well in group situations and take control when I need to. It's not like a dominating thing, with me or with Jake, I just feel comfortable dealing with people. I'm levelheaded. And if there needs to be a leader, I can definitely step up and take over."

That quiet confidence comes naturally to Shawn. It's always been a part of his personality, and it has served him well.

Twin Times

Shawn Robert Ashmore was born on October 7, 1979, in Richmond, British Columbia, to Linda and Rick Ashmore. His birth was cause for a double celebration — Shawn's identical twin, Aaron, arrived as well. Soon after, the family moved to the province of Alberta, where they stayed for ten years. When the twins were eleven, they relocated again, due to Rick Ashmore's job as a manager for a manufacturing company. This time they moved to a suburb of Toronto. That was serendipitous, since that bustling Canadian city is a thriving media center — lots of commercials,

TV shows, and movies are shot there. And by that time, Shawn and Aaron had already started their acting careers.

Shawn explains how it all happened. "When we were living in Alberta, my mom had joined this club for women who had twins or triplets, which was kind of like a community group. And one day, a casting agent came to speak to the group." [The reason: TV shows, movies and especially commercials seek out twins or triplets for baby and young child roles. It's partly because if one child gets cranky, they can substitute the other, but it's also because, by law, babies and small children are only allowed to be in front of the camera for a very limited amount of time. By rotating the twins, that time is doubled.]

Shawn continues, "We were about seven years old. The casting agent asked some of the moms if they would allow their kids to audition for commercials and we said, 'Yeah, why not? That sounds really cool.' So Aaron and I went to our first audition. And he got the part — only he was sick on the day they were filming, so I got to do it. He was kind of upset. But that's how we started."

That was the start all right — not just of the Ashmore twins' career, but of learning to deal with the constant competition, and more importantly, working out a way to feel cool about it. They've had lots of practice.

"Quite often, we've auditioned for the same exact part and one of us has gotten it over the other. So

35

we've had to learn to accept that. We've come to understand that, for some roles, it's not only a 'look' the casting agents have in mind, it's also how you interpret the role. And since Aaron and I have very different personalities, we're bound to do different interpretations. So if his is more along the lines of what they want — he gets the role. If mine is, I do."

Of course, it doesn't always work that way. Sometimes, casting agents really *are* just seeking a specific "look." And if both Shawn and Aaron have it, that could be a problem — actually, it *has* been a problem. "We've gone for commercials," Shawn relates, "and the casting directors have said, 'We like both of you, so we're just going to flip a coin to see which one gets the role. So don't feel bad if you don't get it — it's nothing personal.'"

As it's turned out, both boys have worked pretty much equally. Shawn proudly describes a few of Aaron's impressive roles. "He's done lots of commercials, plus TV shows like *Are You Afraid of the Dark* and *Due South*." Shawn himself has been in such movies as *Fast Track* and *Strike* (with Gaby Hoffmann and Kirsten Dunst); plus the TV movie, *Any Mother's Son,* which aired on cable's Lifetime network.

The big question: Did Aaron also audition for *Animorphs*? Shawn's candid answer: "We did both audition originally." But there were no hard feelings — in fact, Aaron's even been on the show. "There was an episode where there were two Jakes," Shawn says. "We hadn't planned for Aaron to be in it, but he just happened to be visiting the set when we were working on that episode. And we realized that the scene where the two Jakes meet would work better if Aaron played one of them. So he did."

Of course, being a twin wasn't only about competing for acting parts. In fact, neither boy worked often enough to have missed out on a normal childhood. Shawn has strong, mostly happy memories of his. "Having Aaron, I had a best friend, always. In school, we basically had the same interests, so we had a lot of the same classes. If either of us missed an assignment, the other could help out with homework."

They collected baseball and hockey cards together, played video games, and as teenagers, hung out at the mall. Mostly, in the summers, they went skateboarding. "I met a lot of my friends that way," Shawn says. "We'd all go out skateboarding together." In the winters, the group switched to snowboarding, a sport Shawn is still into.

Although some people don't think the boys look identical, others mixed them up all the time. "We didn't have to try to fool people," Shawn says. "It happened by itself. Pranks came to us. There were always teachers who'd give us the wrong report cards, or the wrong tests back. I had one gym teacher who called me Aaron all year long — and that time, he wasn't even in my class. The teacher had him last year, so whenever he saw 'Ashmore' he just assumed it was Aaron again. No matter how many times I corrected him, he still did it."

Shawn's memories include lots of long car trips, mostly for vacations. And that's when sibling rivalry busted out, big time. Shawn remembers with a laugh, "In the car, we were in the backseat and there was this little divider that we'd pull down between us, like an armrest. And we'd split it down the middle — *exactly*. And if I was on his side, even by so much as a hair, or he was on mine, there'd be an argument. But that kind of competition was natural, nothing serious. We're really best friends, we even finish each other's sentences without realizing it."

Shawn and his brother share another talent: They're both musicians. "Aaron and I were in a band for a while," he says. "We both played guitar and wrote songs. We even had a tape out. There was a local label in Toronto that was putting out a compilation CD and they used one of our songs. It's kind of a punk sound — my dad calls it 'jumping around' music. But we also play acoustic guitar and we write blues and flamenco and stuff. We went to music competitions and started playing, and people really liked it, so we did that for a few years."

School Days

In the province of Ontario, where Shawn grew up, high school goes up through grade thirteen — one more year than in the United States. While some kids are less than thrilled about the extra year, Shawn asserts that for him, it was a good thing. "It's a weird system, I know, but I didn't mind doing it. That final year is sort of in between high school and university. It prepares you and gives you extra time to sort of figure out what direction you want to go in."

Most of Shawn's thirteen years at Turner Fenton High School were good ones. Being an avid reader served him well in all his subjects. "The first series of books I got into were the *Chronicles of Narnia*," he says. "It's a fantasy series by C. S. Lewis. That got me into sci-fi and comic books. I went on to read the whole series of *Dune* books after that."

The book that affected him most, however, was *Brave New World.* "That's a book we had to read in school that really hit me. I was like, 'Are you serious?' Just the whole society [author Aldous] Huxley created and how it works, the whole repression thing, being under the control of the government. I can picture it happening, like a nightmare. Plus, being a twin, that book really, really affected me."

Shawn also liked his science courses — especially chemistry, in which he did well. "I like experiments," he relates. "Just dealing with chemicals was fun. Of course, my brother did manage to almost blow up the chem lab one time. He was doing something with sodium and the teacher said not to mix it with water, but he accidentally did and found out what happened — it exploded. But I thought it interesting to learn how atoms work, and how everything is put together, electrons, neutrons, protons. You hear all these terms in the movies and if you haven't taken chemistry, you don't know what they're talking about."

Shawn's least favorite subject? The dreaded math. "I actually did well in it, but I never really liked it." That was the one subject his acting career affected negatively. "I was away doing a movie, and I missed some of the semester so I started falling behind. The worst was word problems — I hated them because I could never get them. I know it's not a big deal, you just work it through step-by-step. But I used to look at it and try to skip steps, and get ahead of myself. I'd miss something in the arithmetic and then I'd get the whole question wrong. But I did finish out the year and got my grade, which is better than a lot of people I know who didn't like it, and just dropped it."

When Shawn graduated high school, his plans were to go to a university in Toronto to study drama and take courses in radio and TV arts. "You learn production and editing techniques and filming and directing techniques. I figured I've been in this business for ten years, so I sort of have a head start in my career. And if I'm not acting, I'd still like to be producing or directing, or doing something else in it."

The "something else" would have to wait. Before Shawn actually got the chance to enroll in college, *Animorphs* came along.

Morphing Into Jake

Because Shawn is close to his character, he never had any real trouble nailing him. But as season one progressed, Shawn became more and more comfortable in his portrayal. "When you start, as an actor, you have an idea how to play the character, but until you find out where the character's going, it's hard. So in the beginning, I read the books, and took my cue from them. But now, I'm using more of myself in creating Jake."

Shawn is enthusiastic about his new costars. "We're all really good friends. We definitely hang out together — on the set and off. We go to malls, movies, out to dinner all together. Once we went to the Indy car races." Of everyone, he's made closest friends with Boris, who plays Marco. "He's the greatest, an amazing actor and a great guy. Like his character, he's hilarious; he really makes you laugh. But he can be serious, someone I could really talk to. I really like everyone, though, and it's great to work with people you really like."

Animal Planet

That said, for Shawn, being around the animals is by far the coolest part of his *Animorphs* experience. "All the animals are trained, but they're still wild. We learned not to make any sudden, quick movements around them, and no running around. But there's always a trainer there and they wouldn't put us in any danger." Still, he confesses, "You never know what they're going to do. Weird stuff is bound to happen." And it does.

Shawn is totally up for telling animal tales.

On the lions: "To mark their territory, lions pee backward — our lion, Bongo, is eight hundred pounds, and that stuff can spray like, twenty feet! If it gets on your clothes, it'll never come out. That has happened a couple of times, but luckily I've never been on the receiving end of the lion's 'gift.'"

On the horses: "They seem to like going to the bathroom when you're doing a take. So you're trying to concentrate and you see stuff out of the corner of your eye. It really used to crack us up when the animals did unexpected things like that, but we've learned to focus and keep it under control."

On the hawk: "The hawks, like all the animals, are trained, but they're still wild. It can be frightening, like when you're standing next to a hungry hawk and you see its claws and big beak. And you think, 'If he thought my finger was a little piece of meat, he might take a chunk out of it.' But nothing like that has happened, and you have to think optimistically."

On the tiger: To *Nickelodeon Magazine,* Shawn told of his scariest moment: "I had to pet a white tiger and [our animal trainer] told me exactly what I could and couldn't do, such as 'Don't move your hand away quickly,' and 'Don't run away, because it'll think you're prey and come after you.' So I started petting the tiger, and somehow it jerked its head — and my fingers went up its nose! I thought, 'If this isn't the time to move my hand away, I don't know what is!' But I also thought, 'If I move my hand away, the tiger will probably bite me,' so I stood there in shock. [Then] I heard the trainer say, 'Back away, back away,' which is what I did. It was kind of cool and funny, but at the time, I was pretty scared."

Shawn Off Camera

Although he's the star of a TV show, Shawn opts to continue living at home with his family. "We have a great relationship," he asserts. He continues to share many of the same interests as his brother. The last book Aaron read, *Rule of the Bone,* is Shawn's current favorite. And the last family vacation they took was a car trip down through the Adirondack Mountains and western New York — where much of that book took place — plus Vermont and New Hampshire. "It was one of the best vacations we ever had," Shawn raved. "We stayed off the interstate highways, and, with no particular plan, just meandered down back roads. We found these amazing little towns and met some really cool people. In one town, we went to a glassblowing studio and sat for hours and watched as craftspeople made vases. It was really, really cool."

When neither Shawn nor Aaron is working, they like to head down to music clubs where their friends often play. "We go and listen to them a lot."

His own musical aspirations have faded somewhat.

"I honestly don't think I'm good enough to continue with music," Shawn assesses. "I know so many people who are better than I am, who dedicate a lot more time to music. So for me, music is what I do to relax. Sometimes when I come home from the set, and I'm stressed out, I'll pick up my guitar and play for ten or fifteen minutes just to get myself relaxed."

Right now, Shawn doesn't have a girlfriend, but he's clear on the kind of girl that attracts him. "Looks are part of it at first, especially a girl's eyes. That draws me to her. But any girl that I would go out with is someone I have to be able to talk to. She has to be funny and smart and nice. Nice is really important."

Shawn doesn't consider being a busy, working actor a hindrance to a relationship. "Sure, I don't have a ton of extra time right now, and sometimes I do work on the weekends, but if I weren't acting, I'd be in school, so it would be kind of the same demands on my time. It's not hard to maintain a relationship — not if you meet the right girl, anyway."

Future Plans

The most imminent plan Shawn has involves an extended vacation he, Aaron, and their friend Chris (not his *Animorphs* costar) have been planning for close to a year. "We're going on a three-month trip to Australia. We'll tour, stay in hostels, learn how to surf, hang out on the beach. I'm so excited about that, I can barely wait. We're planning to stop in Hawaii and in Fiji, too. And we'll take lots of pictures."

College is on the agenda, too. His plans to further his education got postponed, but not canceled. Shawn aims to fit that in when he can.

Professionally, there's no question Shawn wants to stay in acting. He's fully committed to *Animorphs,* but wouldn't turn down a juicy role in a movie, or teleflick if the timing worked out. Right now, he's taking it one step at a time — and having the time of his life.

CHAPTER FOUR

NADIA NASCIMENTO
"Cassie is very spiritual."

Playing the perceptive and caring Animorph, Cassie, is Nadia Nascimento. Cassie is the one who nurtures the others when something is wrong. She's the level-headed one who, even if she doesn't have the solution, is willing to at least *try* something. Cassie is the loving strength that keeps Jake, Rachel, Marco, and Tobias focused on their unasked-for mission: Save Earth from the Controllers and their Yeerk slaves. Though in real life Nadia is not responsible for stopping the alien takeover of the galaxy, she has come to totally understand her on-screen alter ego, Cassie.

"Cassie and I are similar in some ways," Nadia admits. "I think we both think a lot with our heart — too much almost. But I think that makes us both strong people. When Cassie speaks, she's really given it thought before she tells anyone anything. I do that a lot, too. She sits back and listens, but she is always thinking. She doesn't have to say things all the time.

From the Nickel-O-Zone to the superstar zone—here come the amazing *Animorphs* stars. Top row: Chris and Shawn. Bottom row: Nadia, Boris, Brooke.

TOBIAS

Christopher Ralph, who plays Tobias, became an animal lover ever since *Animorphs*.

CASSIE ™

Nadia Nascimento is Cassie: off
camera, she's totally into music.

JAKE

Shawn Ashmore is Jake—in real life, he's into Rollerblading and snow boarding.

RACHEL

Brooke Nevin, who plays Rachel, is 16—she's the youngest cast member.

MARCO

Boris Cabrera is Marco—he's
the only Californian in the bunch.

Animorphs is shot in Toronto, in the studio and on locations such as this one.

Boris and Shawn are buff boys — action scenes help them stay in shape.

Homer is a golden retriever.
In real life, Shawn has one just
like him.

In one episode, there were
two Jakes. Shawn's identical twin,
Aaron, played one of the roles.

Bongo, the lion, is a pro; he's been in a dozen movies. The secret? He's declawed, but his teeth are totally sharp.

It takes six weeks for the special effects department to create each morph!

Once, Chris was an outsider at school—he knows just how Tobias sometimes feels.

There are actually three hawks used in *Animorphs*—they are identical.

When the Andalite Elfangor met Cassie and the gang, he gave them the secret morphing technology.

Like all the animals on *Animorphs*, this croc rocks—and he's real. Cassie morphed into him.

Nadia and Shawn think *Animorphs* is the coolest—they hope the show is on for a long time!

Five strangers, tossed together for a brand-new TV show. Their biggest challenge? To morph into insta-friends on camera as well as off. They did it—now, they rule!

She just knows. She's very spiritual. She is the sweetest girl you'll ever know. Sweet, honest, a true confidant. I think we both love a lot, and we're really caring."

But there are differences between Nadia and Cassie, too — and that's what makes it a fun challenge for Nadia to play the young farm-girl-turned-Animorph. "Cassie is quieter than I am," says Nadia. "She doesn't say a lot of what she feels. I'm out there, totally extroverted. I think constantly and I just say what I'm thinking. Cassie has this restraint, and I just let my guard down and say what I feel. Sometimes I get frustrated with Cassie because we're really so different. I get frustrated that I can't say things — the scripts don't allow it. But I wish I could pull Cassie out in the open. You know, like, 'Come on, girlfriend, tell Jake you love him! Ask him out!'"

Those who know Nadia, especially those who have grown up with her, will tell you that's *exactly* what the young actress would do. Nadia is almost fearless, and takes on all of life's twists and turns as brand-new adventures. And what an adventure *Animorphs* has turned out to be!

"I Was Very Lucky."

Nadia Leigh Nascimento was born on June 7, 1978, in Vancouver, Canada. Her parents, José and Beth, were delighted with their beautiful little girl, whose smile lit up the room. They were determined to shower her with love and understanding. They wanted to protect Nadia, her older brother, Eric, and younger sister, Chantelle, from the cruelties of the world. But they also wanted to make their children strong and unafraid to face life's problems.

The Nascimentos have a diverse background. José and Beth trace their origins from Cape Verde Islands, off the west coast of Africa, and South America. Beth's family is from England. So, automatically, Nadia and Chantelle were *different* from most of their neighbors and friends. But the amazing thing is that Nadia says they never felt that way. "We grew up in *Leave It To Beaver*-land [in] Lynn Valley outside Vancouver. The neighborhood was shaped like a crescent and there were just *so* many kids. All of us kids were, like, the best of friends. All the parents knew each other and we had dinners together and we went camping together. The whole street — like sixty families — would go camping together! The neighborhood was very family oriented. A lot of the kids I grew up with are still my best friends."

Perhaps in some other neighborhood the Nascimentos may have been considered different or outsiders. But not in their Lynn Valley neighborhood. "Chantelle and I were the only black kids on the street," Nadia recalls. "I didn't even notice that until I was pretty much grown up. I think I was about twelve when I realized that I was the only kid that wasn't white. I had this tan all year round — I didn't realize no one else got tan like me. There were never any racial comments or slurs or anything. I was very lucky."

Actually, the Nascimento house was always crowded with neighborhood kids running in and out. "We had an enormous house, and an enormous piece of land," Nadia remembers. "We had this huge ravine in the back. There were so many trees there, too, and down the back there was a trail and a huge stream. Everyone would come to our house to play. We used to go tobogganing down this huge hill in the winter. We had the best time."

Singing the Blues

Nadia is the first to admit that as a child she was very lucky. She was part of a tight-knit and loving family, had lots of friends, and had the opportunity and encouragement to explore her talents. Music was one talent she's been honing since she was just a little girl. At age six, Nadia began taking classical piano lessons; she also studied the violin. In high school, she took up the guitar, and just recently she picked up the harmonica. Some might think the harmonica is a strange instrument to study, but Nadia explains it is a direct connection to America's truest musical form: the blues.

About a year ago, Nadia started studying jazz piano, and that led to her interest in the blues — and the history of the blues. She even discovered the book, *The Land Where the Blues Began*, which is all about the origins of the blues. "If anyone has interest in music, or even race relations, especially in the South, it's a great book to read," says Nadia. "Since I've been playing the blues on my harmonica, I found it to be very inspirational. It was all taken from the Mississippi Delta. If you really know the blues, you'll know these people. They never made it in Hollywood, but they were the [basis] for music. I can see how so much of today's music derives from the blues. It is the beginning of music to me. And it seems lots of people are getting back into the blues. More and more people are playing the harmonica now, too. Like Aerosmith — in the beginning of his songs, Steven Tyler plays old blues songs."

"I Never Thought I Would Be an Actor for the Rest of My Life."

Acting was another interest Nadia pursued, but not until she started Argyle High School. Actually, before high school, Nadia is the first to admit she wasn't much of a student. She was smart enough, but she allowed herself to be distracted. Take math, for example. "I was terrible at it!" insists Nadia. "I had a tutor. My girlfriend and I went to the tutor, and we just ate all the time. We didn't even study. Looking back, I should have studied harder. I could have done well. I had a great tutor, and I was going to a great school. My teacher was willing to help me. But it was just me —

other people can't do it for you. If I had a little more motivation, I could have pulled off an A."

In high school, however, Nadia found the motivation — especially in her drama class. The funny thing is that Nadia initially took drama because, "It was an easy A course. Everyone took theater because you knew you could get an A."

But something unexpected happened. Nadia fell in love with acting, mainly because of her teacher, Mr. Burritt. "He was my acting teacher all through high school," she says. "He taught Jason Priestley [from *Beverly Hills, 90210*] when he was in high school! Mr. Burritt taught us the true fundamentals of being an actor. The first thing is you have to find yourself before you find the character. It's a process.

"At fifteen, you're just hyper. So Mr. Burritt would make us sit down and do yoga and meditate for an hour. We had to find different parts of what was in our [minds] — explore and expand. At the time, we would laugh at him. We'd say, 'Come on, let's do a scene!' We'd mess around. Instead, he said, 'You'll thank me one day when you're doing an audition and some of these breathing exercises I've taught you will help you.' By the end of the first year, I realized, This guy knows something! I wish everyone could take his class. He glows when he walks. He's like a mentor."

Eventually Mr. Burritt suggested that Nadia go out and join a professional theater group. He felt she was very talented and should get some experience outside of school productions.

"I joined a studio called Gastown Actors' Studio," Nadia says. "I took teen courses there, and I did a lot of shows. It was a really nice theater. Talent agents would come to the shows, and I was 'discovered.' I started doing TV, but it was always for fun. I never thought I'd be an actor for the rest of my life. It was just something that was there. It was always an easy A to me. That never changed."

Though acting came easy to Nadia, she never took it for granted. She loved everything about it. Auditioning, reading the script, developing the character — she was putting to use the things Mr. Burritt began teaching her when she was just fifteen. By the time Nadia was seventeen, she had landed a few TV acting jobs, but even today she admits: "My first love will always be theater. It's one hundred percent real. You have to breathe your character. And the audience — you can feed off their energy. If you have a performance and the audience is dead, you really feel it. But when you're feeding off their energy, it's [unbelievable]. I like the interaction, and being able to stay in the character for more than five minutes at a time."

Life Is an Adventure

However, as much as Nadia was excited about acting, she realized something surprising: She wanted to continue her education, too. When she graduated high school, Nadia enrolled in Capilano College and began the transfer program to the University of British Columbia. Her field of interest was sociology. "I have a passion for sociology," she explained shortly after she finished her sophomore year. "The study of society — I love to learn about that. But I don't think I'd actually become a sociology teacher or lecturer, but I study it for my own mind. I've been in college two years now, and I see all these people who are taking courses because they have to. They're paying thousands of dollars and they hate it. They're not talking about what they've learned because it doesn't interest them. But I come home after my classes and say, 'Guess what I found out today?'"

Only weeks after Nadia made that observation, she began filming *Animorphs* in Toronto. And, once again, she found herself changing. She loved every minute of acting, but as she spent months on the set, she found herself fascinated by the behind-the-scenes activity, too. Just as the series was wrapping for hiatus, Nadia was ready to make a change when she got back to school. "I'm going to take some courses in business, to become a producer," she said. "And when I come back to Toronto [for the second season of *Animorphs*], I'm going to take a business program correspondence course."

Another adventure for Nadia!

World Traveler

Ever since she was young, Nadia wanted to explore all the interesting places in the world. She wanted to visit Brazil and West Africa and learn about her family's roots. She wanted to experience new places, new customs, new people. So, in 1997, Nadia started getting some exotic stamps on her passport. She and a friend traveled through Europe for seven months — but not on a timetable. When Nadia found an interesting place, she stayed and investigated all that intrigued her.

One of Nadia's favorite spots was Sintra, Portugal. Located in the middle of the west coast, Sintra is about two hours from Lisbon. Nadia says she found a paradise. "It's the most serene and uplifting place I've ever been," she muses. "It's a utopia in terms of nature, and it had a really good energy to it. The people — oh, my goodness. Sintra is a little town, and all the people wanted to meet us and talk to us. And all the visitors loved it. It was the peak of summer and it was the ideal place. It has the most luscious lake I've ever been to. A lot of celebrities own houses there — like Goldie Hawn and Oprah Winfrey. There are these hills [with so much vegetation] it's like an Amazon jungle. And in the middle of this jungle, right out of the blue, you come across these ancient monasteries. They were built thousands of years ago, but are in prime condition. And right behind a monastery would be Oprah's house. I'd hike through the trees and little paths, eight hours a day. It's like a big exploration. It was beautiful!"

Another high point of Nadia's European adventure was Cappadocia, one of the first Christian settlements in Turkey. "If you like *The Flintstones*, go to Cappadocia," Nadia laughs. "It's like Bedrock — you live in caves there. A huge volcanic eruption from thousands of years ago [created the site] of the city. But [the houses were] caves. Some of them were like five-story buildings. There are staircases inside them, living rooms, bedrooms, and kitchens. The kitchen walls and ceilings are black and charred from cooking in a cauldron. We stayed in the caves. It was like subzero and it was so cold, you felt wet. I'm thinking, 'They have to be heated!' But they weren't. My friend refuses to admit we had pneumonia, but I *know* we did!

"And there are wineries where you can see where they crushed the grapes and fermented the wine. It is absolutely mind-blowing. And it's enormous — like half the size of Toronto. Then there was Rose Valley, where all the rocks were pink — the whole horizon was totally pink! What topped it off was I was in such a good state of mind. I was so happy there."

Nadia also fell in love with Greece during this trip. The architecture, the history, the beauty of the islands impressed her, but she admits the thing she remembers most was the food! "Greek food is my favorite!" she says enthusiastically. "When I was in Europe, I tasted a lot of food — my body can tell you that. I gained thirty pounds. Honey, when I ate, I ate! The way I could tell my favorite place was where I gained the most weight, and I *gained* in Greece. It's the best place to eat. I really liked the calamari, and any kind of potatoes. Their pastries were so nice. And deep-fried cheese. Like I said, I ate *everything*!"

Next on Nadia's trip ticket is South America. She and her boyfriend have planned a south-of-the-equator trip during *Animorphs*' hiatus. "I'm so excited," she said in anticipation of their journey. "Europe is so small, you can go anywhere. South America is so enormous. I *have* to go to Brazil — I have family there. And I have to go to Peru and hike [along] an old Inca trail. That's my main focus — seeing the ruins at Machu Picchu. South America — its history goes back for so long. The things you can see and experience . . . and the spirituality there! It seems like there are ancient ghosts floating around. You *have* to learn something from the experience."

After South America, Nadia wants to check out the African side of her family's legacy. "I want to go to the Cape Verde Islands," she says. "It's off the west coast of Africa. I've always known I would go there someday. Ever since I was a kid, that's where I wanted to go. The people there are golden! It's beautiful, and I have family there, though I've never met them. My dad has brothers and sisters there, and I have lots of cousins there. I want to see where my dad came from."

Indeed, for Nadia, life is one big adventure reaching out for her to experience. She seems to grow with each new bend in the road. Right now, she is thrilled to be part of the *Animorphs* team.

"I Love My Friends."

Several days before the *Animorphs* set was due to close for hiatus, Nadia was chronicling all the things she wanted to do during the break. But she also admitted that she was going to really miss her new friends, Brooke, Christopher, Boris, and Shawn. "I love my friends," she enthused. "I really love them. It's so lucky for me — I have an individual relationship with each of them. We each have specific ties between us. Brooke, the only other chick . . . we have a great friendship. Actually, she was the one I was worried about, because she was the only other girl and there's a huge age difference between us. She's younger than my sister, and you know, there's that whole 'little sister' thing. I'm thinking, 'If she's younger than Chan, then this [is] going to be death.' I didn't think we would have *anything* in common. What I found out was she's so much more mature than I am. She's the kind of person who tells me to calm down. She's like my mom — almost. But then, I give her a lot of advice, so I'm like her mom. Actually, I shouldn't say mom — it's not really *that* kind of relationship.

"And Boris — we have a great relationship. We're both away from home — I'm from Vancouver and he's from Los Angeles. So we started off together in the hotel. We were 'homeless,' and we didn't know anyone. That's one thing [that brings people together] — when you don't know anyone, it's scary and you can't hide that. So I think that's where the friendship started. Shawn, Chris, and I — we're about the same age. Chris didn't have as many scenes as the rest of us this season, but Shawn and I worked a lot together. We have the same social background, too. But all of us have such laughs together — it's incredible."

"We Have a Lot to Learn From Each Other."

The *Animorphs* cast members weren't the only ones who noticed the magic link between them. The producers, directors, and the rest of the crew quickly became aware of the bond the five had developed. It was obvious on and off screen. "[The producers] are very happy about the way it's worked out," Nadia explains. "Regardless of age or anything else, we are all very individual, we're so disgustingly dissimilar, but we get along. We have a lot to learn from each other. You meet everyone for a reason, right? Even if it's only to meet them on the street for five minutes, there's a reason you talk to them. And these guys — it's very definite why I met them: I'm learning a lot from them. *I'm so lucky — I love my costars!*"

Nadia's not the only lucky one. *Animorphs* fans are feeling pretty fortunate to have made her acquaintance, too!

CHAPTER FIVE

BORIS CABRERA

"Marco hurts a lot inside."

Boris Cabrera is the laugh-a-minute Marco. He is the one who always has some wisecrack or comment when the Animorphs are planning their skirmishes with the Controllers and Yeerks. He is the one who actually came up with the word "Animorphs." And, though Tobias is the mysterious one, there's something strange going on back at Marco's home with his dad, Jeremy.

As for Marco's real-life "host" — Boris Cabrera — well, a lot is going on there, too. "The only similarity I have with Marco is that we both like to make people laugh," asserts Boris. "But Marco is also the one who's most cautious. He's the one who says, 'Let's think about this. What if this happens?' He thinks about consequences. Everyone else wants to jump into things, but Marco likes to use his common sense."

But there's another side of Marco — a very sad

side that he tries to hide with his wisecracks and jokes. "Marco hurts a lot inside," says Boris. "He doesn't show it much. The only person who knows Marco's pain is his best friend, Jake. Marco's trying to get over the loss of his mom. Marco is very insecure because his mom is gone. Then, there is his father — Marco hardly gets any attention from him, so there's a lot of insecurity there, too. Marco is still trying to find himself. Besides dealing with the death of his mom, he has to deal with everyday life. He wants to make sure his friends like him; that's probably the most important thing to Marco. So he hides all his pain and sorrow through his jokes. That happens a lot."

Pain and sorrow — that's where the reel-life and the real-life of Boris Cabrera really go off into opposite directions!

"Our Neighborhood Was Not So Good."

Boris Alberto Cabrera was born on December 16, 1980, in Inglewood, California. His parents, George and Eugenia Cabrera, welcomed this early Christmas present to their little family, which already included their first son, Arturo. George worked as a handyman and Eugenia stayed at home and took care of the boys. The family moved to Pacoima, California, when Boris was still just a baby. Proud of their Hispanic heritage, the Cabreras followed their cultural tradition of the family being the solid base of everything else. They knew it was their responsibility to teach their children about integrity, loyalty, and morality. Boris explains that his parents created an atmosphere of love and encouragement in their home. This established a special security for Arturo and Boris. That was very important since on the other side of the Cabreras' front door was a very dangerous world.

Boris explains that his childhood neighborhood was not the *Leave It To Beaver*-land that Nadia Nascimento grew up in. No way! As a matter of fact, Boris admits that not only was it hard to grow up in his southern California neighborhood, but it was even impossible for some to live long enough to grow up. "Our neighborhood . . . was not so good," he says. "There were gangs. I lived right around the corner from a gang."

Many of Boris's neighborhood friends ended up involved with gangs. "When you're young it's hard," Boris says. "It's hard to stay away from gangs in a neighborhood like mine. When all your friends are outside, you want to be outside and hang with them, too. . . . A lot of times, [kids] join a gang because they need to be wanted, to be [a part of something]. Supposedly [the gang] becomes your family, because you're with them more than your own family."

However, Boris never fell for that particular temptation. First of all, he saw the basic lie about gang life. "It's not good," insists Boris. "You come to realize after a while that when you go outside to see your gang friends, you're going to do the same thing that day, the next day, and the next day, and so on. It gets boring. . . . [Plus] you don't really have friends in a gang. You're on your own."

But the most important reason Boris and his brother, Arturo, refused to wear gang colors and hang out their lives away was George and Eugenia Cabrera. "My brother and I found better things to do with our time than to join a gang," Boris recalls. "My parents had a great deal to do with it. If they hadn't done their job as parents, like give us the attention we needed, we would have definitely been on the streets every day. . . . Instead, my parents encouraged us to always stay busy. My brother was always an honor student, so he was always in his room hitting the books. I surrounded myself with sports. I became a wrestler and competed at school."

If there was ever a question in Boris's mind about joining a gang, it was dismissed the first time (and unfortunately not the last time) that he saw a friend get shot. "Losing friends — that was the scariest thing about living around gangs," Boris admits sadly.

George and Eugenia Cabrera were determined to keep their sons safe from the dangerous streets. But even they never dreamed that Boris would become an actor. Because Boris was so involved in sports, they thought he might pursue a career in that particular field. He also showed that he had picked up his father's skill in repairing things around the house. Boris has a natural talent working with cars, and when he's back home in California, you can usually find him restoring his vintage 1966 cherry-red Mustang. "It's an awesome car," Boris says proudly. "I learned about cars by taking it apart and putting it back together, with a new part, just the way I saw it. I'm pretty handy like my dad. I learned everything because of him. I grew up being a perfectionist. When I do things, they're usually done right or not at all. I've redone the whole motor already, and now I'm going to start on the exterior and interior."

"I Didn't Take It Seriously."

Growing up, Boris was all boy. He liked "boy" things — sports, cars, cracking jokes. "I never wanted to be an actor," Boris now laughs. "As a kid, I thought acting was stupid, that it was a dumb idea. Then, when I was eleven, my godfather introduced me to acting, and everything changed.

"I was at a family party, and I was dancing. As a kid, I would never play with the other kids at a party. Running around, popping balloons, that wasn't me. I liked to dance! For some reason, I was always different. I was the one who liked to dance and talk to girls . . . So I was dancing at this party, and a friend of my father's, Rolando Molina, came over to me and said, 'Come here, man.' I thought I was in trouble! I was like, 'I swear I wasn't doing anything! Am I in trouble?'"

Rolando, who was a close friend of the Cabrera family, laughed and assured Boris everything was fine, that he just wanted to talk to him about something.

Boris still remembers the mix of feelings he had when Rolando asked him if he ever considered being an actor, if he would like to be in a TV show or a movie. "I didn't really take it seriously," Boris admits, "but I told him, 'Yeah, I'd like to try.' He gave me the phone number of a talent agency and told me to call. I made an appointment and I met this woman who had me read from a script. I was numb. I didn't believe it until I actually booked my first audition — it was for a Coca-Cola commercial. I was so nervous, I was shaking like crazy, but I got the part anyway. It was great, pretty cool."

Sounds like a plot from a movie? Well, it's even better than that! It's almost a Steven Spielberg feel-good movie! You see, Rolando Molina was not *always* into acting. For years he was a security guard at Universal Studios. He would check the actors, the studio executives, and employees in and out as they drove on and off the studio lot. One of the familiar faces Rolando saw every day was actor Edward James Olmos. "He would always be polite to Mr. Olmos," Boris says as he tells the often repeated story. "Mr. Olmos would always come through the gate and Rolando would say, 'Hello, Mr. Olmos.' And then, Mr. Olmos would say to him, 'It's Eddie, call me Eddie.' So they became friends. Then, Mr. Olmos was doing the film *American Me*, and he told Rolando that there was an extra part in it for him if he wanted it. That's how Rolando got started as an actor. A few weeks later, he told Mr. Olmos, 'I don't know how to repay you, Eddie.' And Mr. Olmos said, 'Do the same thing I did for you for another Latino kid, that's how you can repay me.'"

Boris was the recipient of Edward James Olmos' pass-along favor. Boris realized what a special gift Rolando had received from the socially conscious actor, and even as a preteen Boris was determined to be the best he could. "Rolando and I got really close after that," Boris says. "He's my acting coach now — he's such a talented man. I asked him to be my sponsor at my First Communion, so that's why I call him my godfather."

"My Favorite Part of Learning Is Everyday Life."

Boris worked very hard at his acting. He studied, he auditioned, and he won some roles and lost some. The important thing was that Boris didn't give up when he didn't get a role. He just got more determined. Okay, Boris is not a super-saint — he admits if he doesn't get a part or hasn't worked in a while, a certain amount of, well, "panic" sets in. But that's natural, because growing as an actor means a lot to him now.

After the Coca-Cola commercial, Boris worked steadily. He appeared in numerous commercials, and guest-starred in such TV series as *Pacific Blue*, *Charlie Grace*, *ER*, and *Walker, Texas Ranger*. He also appeared on stage in the play *Christmas at Vaughn Street*, and costarred in the HBO film *August Fires*.

When Boris wasn't on location, he was back in school, studying hard to keep his grades up, and also making himself a star in a whole other field — sports. Boris played on his school team or community team in soccer, football, baseball, and even competitive Ping-Pong. He earned his purple belt in karate, and was named California State High School Champion Wrestler in 1997.

As the first season of *Animorphs* headed into hiatus, Boris was studying with his own tutor and just finishing up his junior year courses. Actually, Boris prefers studying with a tutor to attending regular school. He feels the personal attention and the hands-on work with a tutor really helps him learn. You see, Boris confesses that he's not the biggest fan of the organized drill of reading, writing, and arithmetic. "I'm not exactly fond of [school]," he says candidly. "My favorite part of learning is everyday life. Most of my knowledge comes from that. [Regular] school is too easy; it's not a challenge to me, and it becomes boring."

Boris's tutor understands how his pupil feels, and he has constructed their study sessions to reflect that. Whether it's obvious or not, everything they do together turns out to be a learning experience. They fool around surfing the Net on the computer and before he knows it, Boris has found out how to research an English paper. A Saturday outing to a museum turns out to be a hands-on study in art history.

This real-life approach has helped Boris understand the importance of getting a well-rounded education. "I need my high school diploma," Boris explains. "Regardless if it's hard or easy, you have to get it — right? So I'm doing that. I'm doing what I need to do so I can concentrate on my career as an actor. I want to entertain people — that's what I do best. So I'm going to do my best in the things that will bring me to that point."

"What's an Animorph?"

Right now, Boris feels *Animorphs* is his career's big break. As a matter of fact, Boris admits that right before he landed the role of Marco, he was getting a little nervous. His last project had been his guest role on *Walker, Texas Ranger* in February 1998. By March, Boris was getting antsy about not getting another role, so when his agent called him to audition for this new show called *Animorphs,* the young actor was really excited. "I knew I had to get this part," he reveals. "So I went a day early to get the sides [actor-speak for script pages of the scenes he would be doing]. I studied them and started playing with the character. I was trying to figure him out, but it was hard. *Animorphs?* What is that all about?"

Boris went to Rolando Molina and asked him to help him prepare for his audition. He was determined to get the part of Marco. What Boris didn't know was that the *Animorphs* producers were just as determined to find the right Hispanic actor to play Marco. And they were on an up-against-the-wall time schedule because production was set to start in Toronto in a matter of days. Another actor had originally been cast as Marco, but he was injured in an accident shortly before production was to start. That's when emergency calls were made to California agents "to find Marco!"

When Boris read for the producers, he had no idea there was so much pressure on them. Maybe that was lucky, because that would have made him even more nervous! But, no matter, Boris auditioned and nailed the role. The producers knew they had found Marco. The next thing Boris thought was "Oh, God! I'm on a plane! I'm going to Canada! It was so all of a sudden."

The Meaning of Friendship

Even though Boris was thrown into the middle of the *Animorphs* production later than the rest of the cast, he was soon at ease in his new surroundings. The main reason for this easy transition was his fellow actors — Nadia, Shawn, Christopher, and Brooke. "I feel very fortunate to be working with this cast," Boris enthuses. "They are all professionals. They all know exactly what they are doing. It's awesome, and it makes my job so much easier."

In spite of the age range and background differences, Boris, Nadia, Shawn, Christopher, and Brooke found themselves depending on each other, both on and off screen. And, like his character, Marco, Boris was the "funny guy." Also like his character, Boris found he had really bonded with Shawn. As Animorphs, Marco and Jake are best friends. And only weeks into production Boris found himself admitting, "I [consider] Shawn my best friend. He's great — I like him a lot. He's got a good sense of humor, and he's very open-minded, which I like in a person. Besides that, we have the most scenes together, so on a professional level, you want to get along with the person you're working with every day. If he's easy to get along with, you usually start hanging out with him outside of work. Shawn and I do a lot of things together. Shopping, the movies, hanging out with each other."

The irony is that if you had asked Boris a week before he landed the role of Marco, who his best friend was, there would have been no way he would have described anyone like Shawn. Quite candidly, Boris admits that coming from a Latino neighborhood, he didn't really know many "Anglo" kids, much less one from Toronto, Canada! "Where I'm from, there aren't many white people," Boris admits quite candidly. "So I didn't know how to react to [Shawn], or how to speak around him."

Well, Boris got over that quickly. Labels and preconceptions were forgotten almost immediately and Boris and Shawn soon realized they laughed at the same things, enjoyed doing the same things, and even had a similar approach to life. They liked each other, but more important they trusted each other, and that allowed them to be themselves with each other. They even were able to turn those initial "differences" into a running joke. "Shawn's cool," explains Boris. "I call him 'white boy.' I can call him that and he's like, 'Wassup, Boris?' It's like, dude, you're cool. He's like, 'That's what I am, right?' . . . We're pretty bad sometimes. We'll sit around and talk [trash] at each other all day. It's fun to do that with someone you get along with."

The point is, that Boris and Shawn are actually making fun of the labels some people use to set themselves apart from others. Their attitude makes stereotypes and labels meaningless and harmless. Boris and Shawn respect one another's backgrounds and traditions, but best of all, they found they can make one another crack up. That's true friendship.

And It Continues . . .

Animorphs means a lot to Boris. It's not only a major step in his career, and it not only introduced him to new people and a best friend. But *Animorphs* has also given Boris a very important opportunity — some day he may be in the position to carry on the tradition started by Edward James Olmos. You see, success for Boris will not only mean fame and fortune for Boris, but it will mean he will be able to reach out to the Latino community and help another boy or girl achieve their dream.

CHAPTER SIX

MEET THE ANIMAL STARS OF ANIMORPHS

"People do not understand animals anymore."

There's an old belief in Hollywood that an actor never wants to costar with a little child or an animal. Why? Well, because no matter how fine an actor you are, the cute child or the animal is going to upstage you. You might be in the middle of a dramatic scene or even a sidesplitting comic scene, and inevitably the child or animal is going to do something to draw attention away from you. No matter how well the scene is planned and directed, it *always* seems to happen.

If this is true — what were the producers of *Animorphs* thinking?! After all, the stars, Nadia, Boris, Chris, Brooke, and Shawn, are all kids, and their weekly costars are definitely the animals they morph into. According to Hollywood tradition, isn't that a formula for disaster? "We knew that a major challenge with the show would be getting real, wild animals and we were very lucky to find Michael Hackenberger, who had all the lions, tigers, wolves, and other spectacular creatures that we needed to make the show really exciting. And even better, he had lots of experience in film and television," says Deborah Forte, executive producer of *Animorphs.*

Perhaps because *Animorphs* was already breaking tradition with its high-tech morphing effects, no one ever gave the animal theory a second thought. As a matter of fact, according to *Animorphs* co-executive producer, Bill Siegler, they searched for and found Canada's *best* animal resource — the Bowmanville Zoo, which is located just outside of Toronto. "Our line producer, Lina Cordina, knew Michael Hackenberger of the Bowmanville Zoo from his work on the film *The Ghost in the Darkness*, and she knew he was one of the best," says Siegler.

When the *Animorphs* producers met with Michael, certain ground rules about the animals were established right away. They all agreed not to use endangered animals on the show. "We don't think it would be right," explained Siegler. "First of all, they are hard to find and to work with. But more important than that, to exploit [their condition] wouldn't be right."

When Michael understood where the *Animorphs'* people were coming from, he had no second thoughts about the Bowmanville Zoo working with the show. He knew his animals would be treated with love and respect.

"You Learn Just By Being Around Animals."

The Animorphs — Jake, Rachel, Cassie, Marco, and Tobias — morph into lots of different animals. On the show, Jake's main alter animal is a dog, but during the show's first season, he transformed into a cockroach, a butterfly, a lobster, and a tiger. Rachel's usual animal persona is the lion, though she has taken the form of a housefly, a cat, a cockroach, and a butterfly. Marco's personal animal form is the rat, but he's turned into a python, a cockroach, and a butterfly. Cassie is best known for changing into a horse, but she's assumed the body of a rabbit, a skunk, a butterfly, a crocodile, and a cockroach. And, finally, there's the mysterious Tobias — for the first season, he mainly took the form of a hawk.

The Bowmanville Zoo is the permanent home of the *Animorphs*' lion, horse, python, and hawks. Some other Bowmanville Zoo residents have also appeared as "extras" on the series — including tigers and elephants. As director (and owner) of the Bowmanville Zoo, Michael Hackenberger is devoted to the care and health of the animals there. Actually, working with and protecting animals has been a lifelong vocation for Michael. He remembers that even as a child, he knew he had a special bond with animals. "When I was four years old, I was drawing pictures of myself working with animals," the forty-two-year-old Michael says. "It really is a gift. There are people who have mathematical gifts or musical gifts. My gift happens to be with animals. And, like any gift, you never take it for granted, and you try to nurture and develop it."

When Michael was seventeen, he ran away and joined a circus. Really! It was the Garden Brothers Circus, and his job was to shovel elephant manure. It may not have been glamorous, but Michael insists it was a perfect way to learn about animals. "You learn just by being around them," he says. "You really [pick up] what the animals tell you."

After traveling with the circus, Michael returned to school and earned a college degree in zoology and a graduate degree in animal science. When Michael got out into the real world, he was drawn to jobs where he could work one-on-one with animals. It was natural for him to train animals for films and TV. In 1987, he had an opportunity of a lifetime — to buy the Bowmanville Zoo, which had originally opened in 1919 and was Canada's oldest operating zoo. "The former owner was getting on in age, and he wanted to retire," Michael explains. "He'd put his entire life into it, and it's a very demanding situation."

Welcome to the Bowmanville Zoo

For the next ten years, Michael, his wife, Wendy, who is the zoo vet, and a handful of caretakers and trainers, totally renovated Bowmanville Zoo. Now, every facility is new and totally animal-friendly. As a matter of fact, the whole atmosphere of the Bowmanville Zoo is dedicated to keeping the animals happy and thriving. But it is also important to Michael that zoo visitors walk away with more than stats and facts about the animals there. "The essential philosophy we have at the zoo is that there is an animal apartheid, that people do not understand animals anymore," says Michael. "I've reached the point where I don't care if people leave the zoo knowing an elephant weighs eight thousand pounds and eats two hundred pounds of food and drinks fifty gallons of water a day. I want people to come to the zoo and look at an elephant and experience it emotionally, to think, 'What a tremendous animal.' What it weighs is not as important as understanding the kinship animals have with us, that they share this planet with us. That's the bottom line. And if the only message people get when they come to Bowmanville is that, then we've done our job."

Bowmanville Zoo visitors do come away with a unique experience — mainly because, unlike most zoos, it is very hands-on. "Most zoos do not allow public feeding of the animals," Michael explains. "We do. We have a herd of deer that are loose in the zoo, and people can approach them, and see them without cages. We have elephant rides. We have shows throughout the day specifically geared toward interaction between humans and animals."

Meet Bongo and His Friends

Bowmanville Zoo's reputation spread throughout the animal training industry, and soon film and TV production companies wanted to tap into such a rich resource. About five years ago, Michael started using some of Bowmanville's residents in films. They did a number of difficult location films in Africa, and word spread fast. "We've done *The Ghost in the Darkness*, *George of the Jungle*, and *Urban Legend* — we had rats in *Urban Legend*," Michael says. "Those are just the recent ones. I mean, we have one lion here, Bongo, who's been in over fifteen feature films."

Actually, Bongo is the favorite animal of most of the *Animorphs*' cast. Bongo seems to have quite a personality. "It's always fun when Bongo comes," says Nadia, "because we *know* something's going to happen. He makes us laugh because he's so smart. During every rehearsal, he'll do things properly. He doesn't start charging and eating all the directors! We'll rehearse about ten times, and he nails it every time. Then the second we say, 'Roll film!' I think he laughs and says, 'I'm gonna mess them up.' So every time the camera starts, Bongo goes the other way, or he sprays someone. Sprays — like a male cat — you know. Yuck!"

Brooke seconds Nadia's vote for Bongo being the coolest animal costar. That's good because Brooke's character, Rachel, is most often morphed into a lion. Take a breath when Brooke starts to extol Bongo's attributes: "He's amazing! The first time I saw Bongo, I was so taken aback because he was the most beautiful lion I had ever seen — especially close up. His eyes, his magnificent mane! I definitely have deep respect for Bongo, but I won't say I wasn't scared or anything. It was really exciting — especially when in one of the shots I had to walk about a foot away from him. I was in the cage with Bongo — but Michael, the trainer, was there, just out of the shot [just to be safe]. It was amazing. I was *so* close to that lion!"

Bongo is twelve years old, and was born at the Bowmanville Zoo. According to Michael, he's not old, but if he lived in the wild, Bongo would probably be dead by now. "When a male lion is in charge of a pride," Michael explains, "he generally loses that edge he needs to stay in control by the time he reaches the age of ten. A five- or six-year-old male lion will [push] a ten-year-old lion out of the pride. When that happens, a lot of times the older lion is killed."

Thankfully, Bongo is alive and well at Bowmanville, and slyly leaving his mark on the set of *Animorphs*. But while Nadia thinks Bongo's visits are fun, Shawn isn't so sure. "Bongo is declawed," Shawn says. "But he's eight hundred pounds — he's a huge animal! It's not exactly scary, but sometimes [I'm] concerned around wild animals. We have to be careful. No quick movements and no running around. Of course, there's always a trainer there. They wouldn't put us in danger."

Come Fly With Me

Shawn is also a little hesitant when it comes to the hawks used when the character Tobias morphs.

"What's scary is standing next to a hungry hawk," insists Shawn. "You see his claws and big beak. If he thought my finger was a little piece of meat, he could take a chunk out of it. Of course, that's never happened."

What has happened is a bit less threatening — at least for Chris, who plays Tobias and works with the hawk the most. Actually, there are three hawks from Bowmanville used in *Animorphs*. There's Hera, Cesaer, and Tobias. "I met Hera first," Christopher recalls. "I think he's the one I have most contact with. I guess they use 'double' hawks because some can fly better or look better. Anyway, there are three of them, and each one has the same tendency to relieve himself when we're shooting. Every take!"

Besides being, well, messy, it can be annoying, especially when Chris is doing the time-consuming green-screen morphing sequence with the hawk. Before they even started shooting *Animorphs*, Chris says the cast spent several weeks getting to know the animals. It allowed the animals to feel comfortable with the actors, and it allowed the cast to study the animals' movements. "After staring at the animal for hours, you pick up its movements," Chris says. "Not that someone is going to mistake me for a hawk, but I kind of clumsily imitate it."

Except when it has to take a bathroom break!

Nadia's Tale of the Lion or the Horse

As for Nadia, well, you know she's the daring one of the group. She loves Bongo the lion, and even admits that she is "infatuated with him. I think it's an honor to work with him." Nadia feels that they have a special bond because both of their original roots go all the way back to Africa. "We're from the same place," she explains.

However, even Nadia admits the first time she worked with Bongo, her natural fears suddenly appeared. "I did flip out a little when I [did a scene] with Bongo," she recalls. "I thought he was going to eat my back — I swear. He was sniffing my back. Now, I know my butt is tempting, but. . . . Then the trainers started giving him kibble. And I'm thinking, 'But what if he wants a rump roast?!' But he didn't eat me. [I think he recognized] our bond. We're brother and sister!"

The surprising thing is that big, brave, Bongo-loving Nadia admits, "I'm more scared to work with Foxfire, the horse. Once, I got chucked by the horse, and it really scared me. He kicked my leg, and I had this huge horseshoe print on my thigh. Horses make me shake a little now. But I'm glad I'm the horse — [because] I don't have to ride it. I don't have to get on that thing! I love looking at horses, maybe touching their noses, but I can't throw my leg over the top of them now."

Elephant Walk

And then there's Boris. He's in heaven with the animals on *Animorphs*. You can barely get him away from Jesse, the dog. "He's the golden retriever that Jake turns into at the beginning of the show," says Boris. "I love that dog. I'm always playing with him — he's really friendly. He listens, which makes you like him even more."

Just as with the other cast members, Boris was pretty impressed with Bongo the lion. "He's a big sweetheart," insists Boris. "A big kitty cat. But, still, look at the size of him. It's overwhelming. He [always] wants to play with you. But he'll barely tap you and you'll fly — and he's *just* cuddling!"

Another time, Boris was doing some publicity shots with his castmates at the Bowmanville Zoo. The photographer had them stand in front of the elephants. Simple enough, right? Well, when the cast lined up, the fun began. "We were about twenty feet in front of the elephants," Boris says. "So we [started] taking pictures, and I felt something pushing my back. [I turned around] and saw it was an elephant. There was this *huge* trunk in my face. So I stepped back, and he kept pushing his trunk out, reaching for me. I put my arm up, and he reached out to touch [my hand] with his trunk. It was the neatest thing I've ever experienced in my life. Here was this two-ton animal, reaching out to me, and I'm reaching out to him. I could feel him breathing on my fingers!"

Boris became even more fascinated by the elephants when, one day, he saw Michael Hackenberger's three-year-old son, Kurt, playing with one of the elephants. "It was incredible," Boris asserts. "When the boy gets near, the elephant makes this really loud clicking noise. I'm not lying — I never thought an elephant could make such a noise. Then the boy stands between this thing's [front] legs, and the elephant caresses him with her trunk. She loves this little boy."

Michael explained the unusual relationship between Kurt and Limba the elephant. It seems that Limba, an Indian elephant, had lived her entire thirty years of life in a small zoo outside Quebec. There were no other elephants, and she had little social interaction with the caretakers. Limba was in bad shape. She was so skinny that she looked as if she were starving. When Michael heard about her, he made arrangements to bring her back to the Bowmanville Zoo to nurse her back to health. She was so emaciated, that the vet at the Quebec zoo didn't think Limba would live through the trip back down to Toronto.

Happily, Limba made it home with Michael, and he and his crew began feeding her favorite foods to fatten her up. Though Limba responded to the nourishment, she was still very shy and sad. She had lived her whole life in a pen. Everything seemed to scare her — she didn't even know what a puddle of water was! And then, there were the *other* elephants at Bowmanville. They were African elephants, who by nature are more rambunctious than Indian elephants. Their antics only frightened Limba even more. Then, one day Michael's son, Kurt, was playing by the elephants. "Here was this goofy little kid and this wonderful thing happens," Michael recalls. "This elephant falls in love with him. Now she is just totally besotted with him. If she sees him, she tries to climb under the pen. She'll start bellowing and throwing a stick at him to get his attention. He goes over to play with her, and she follows him around like a dog. What this has done for Limba is neat. It's given her a lot of self-confidence. So she's far more comfortable with the other elephants now. Her quality of life has shot up as a result of her relationship with Kurt. I've been around elephants a long time, and I've never seen anything like this. But it's really wonderful to see what's happening. Kurt will say, 'Come here, Wimba, let's go for a walk,' and off they go. It's very touching. I have another son, Dirk. He's twenty months, and Limba likes him, but she's not gaga over him like she is with Kurt. I can't explain it. And, to me, I don't need to. I just accept it for what it is — a beautiful relationship."

And, guess what — *you* might just be able to see Limba during *Animorphs*' second season. Now that would be cool!

CHAPTER SEVEN

How'd They Do That?
Those Amazing Special Effects

"I watched my arms become paws. It didn't hurt."
— Jake, on his first morph into Homer

The Rules of the Morph

1. Once an Animorph has **TOUCHED AN ANIMAL,** acquiring and copying its unique DNA pattern, the Animorph may become that animal at any time.

2. An Animorph can only move from **HUMAN TO ANIMAL AND BACK TO HUMAN,** never from one animal to another.

3. An Animorph cannot **TOUCH** another Animorph and thereby acquire his or her **ANIMAL PATTERN**.

4. In a morph, an Animorph must **CONTROL THE ANIMAL MIND,** which can tempt a cat to chase a mouse, or cause a horse to panic at loud noises. In the animal state, **THE HUMAN MIND REMAINS INTACT** and must prevent the animal

from becoming distracted from the mission at hand.

5. The Animorphs can **COMMUNICATE MENTALLY** with one another through telepathy or **THOUGHT-SPEAK** but only when in close contact, not over vast distances.

6. **MORPHING IS VERY TIRING**. Animorphs should generally wait as much as an hour before morphing again, though Cassie, especially gifted at morphing, can sometimes do it in as little as **TEN MINUTES**.

7. Most important, an Animorph must not remain in animal form longer than **TWO HOURS,** or he or she will be trapped there . . . **PERMANENTLY**.

So goes the morph code that Jake, Rachel, Cassie, Marco, and Tobias must live by when a mutating moment becomes necessary. Those scenes alone make *Animorphs* the coolest show on the tube. Watching human eyes elongate, mouths mutate, facial features fully transform, hands and feet change into paws or claws, is mind-blowing. Those bone-crunching sounds and squishy slurps as the kids change shape makes it all the more eerie. Even the actors, who are totally used to it now, still get a buzz out of it.

Shawn says, "Seeing it for the first time was kind of weird. I saw the one where I turn into Homer for the first time, in the tunnel. I saw it in stages, which wasn't as powerful as seeing it on TV. Once you know the technique, it's not as 'wow!' But it really is amazing when you watch it on TV. They do a great job on the effects."

So . . . ever wonder just how they do that great job? And how they make it all look and sound so real? Hint: Morphing involves a combination of high-tech hijinks *and* "how-low-can-you-go-tech" — like a bag of pretzels.

Check it out: The mysteries of the morph are about to be revealed.

It's a Green-Screen Thing

The actors and animals may get most of the attention, but it takes hundreds of talented folks who work behind the scenes to make *Animorphs* come to life each week.

One of them is Sue Sheridan. Her title is visual effects post production supervisor. Translation: She heads up one of the teams responsible for much of what's done to the film after the actors — human and animal! — have completed their parts.

That includes many of the special effects, or f/x as it's called in showbiz lingo. In a show like *Animorphs*, that's a daunting job.

The Rules of the Special Effects Morphing

1. **Do not wear anything — or *be* — green**. "To shoot a morph scene, we use a room, or studio, that's totally green. Green material is draped on the walls,

and the floors are green, too. We chose green since it's one color that is not found on the human body, or on too many animals. That's because, later on, with a computer, that color will be erased from the scene. That way, we end up with our actor posed against *no background at all,* and we can insert our own background. We can make it night or day; we can 'place' the hawk in a forest. For that reason, the actor may not wear any item of clothing that's green, or it, too, will disappear. When we need to use a green animal, like a lizard or crocodile, we switch to a blue room."

2. **Say cheese — not.** When the actors come to the green-screen studio for their morph scenes, they must try and pose like the animal they're being morphed into. That's so Sue and her team can shoot the film, and later, on dual computer monitors, freeze each frame — the human will be on one screen, the animal on another. Then they line up the person's eyes with the animal's eyes; nose with the nose — or beak, as the case may be — hands with paws and so on. Sue says, "We use a Magic Marker to outline each feature, and frame by frame, slowly change the shape to match that of the animal. So if we're morphing Jake into Homer, we'll line up their eyes and, frame by frame, Jake's eyes will become rounder, his nose wider, his mouth will elongate into Homer's snout. We do it in pieces. The name of the computer program we use is called Elastic Reality."

3. **Cassie, the crocodile; a hawk named Jake.** "For instance, take the episode where Cassie morphed into the crocodile. We shot the crocodile in profile, then Nadia came in and posed in the exact same profile. Using the computers, we elongated her mouth and nose about six inches. Then, we drew scales up her back, changed her hands to crocodile feet, and, later, replaced all the drawings with real crocodile skin. The hawk is difficult because they don't have many features that are similar to humans. When Chris, who plays Tobias, comes in, he has to imitate the hawk's movements, move his head in a jerky way like the hawk does. It's a challenge."

4. **Animals first!** "Because it's harder to shoot the animals — they're trained, but they're wild — we usually green-screen them first. It's hard to get them to stand still in the best of scenarios, but in a green studio with hot lights and forty crew members standing around, they're easily distracted. It takes about an hour or two to get one shot of one animal for morphing." It's only after the animal has been filmed that the corresponding human comes in and poses like his or her animal.

5. **The bigger, the better.** "The special effects technology that allows us to create the human-to-animal and back-again morph works best with larger animals. That's why we like to use the lion, tiger, wolf, horse, and the dog so often."

6. **Rats to the rats.** "The smaller the animal, the harder it is to create the effect," Sue says. "Rats are really difficult, because they can't stay still long enough to be filmed. They're skittish; they dart around; their noses are always moving. Increasing the speed of the camera helps, but in general, it doesn't really work. The end result never looks as good as when you do larger animals." That's precisely why, in the episode where Marco and Jake morphed into mice, or Rachel into the cockroach, you didn't see the actual morph.

7. **Human-to-Andalite morphs rule.** "The best-looking morphs, from a special effects point of view, are the human-to-Andalite morphs," Sue says, "because there are more similarities in shape — and just seeing a human distorted into an alien is really interesting. We can do more, we can make the skin turn blue, the eyes turn red. There's more freedom than when you have to match an actual animal." The über-morph, from her point of view, was the episode where the Andalite Ax acquired the DNA and morphed through each of the *Animorphs* kids — he had Marco's hair and eyes, Rachel's face. "We were able to 'create' a completely new person," she marvels.

8. **Pretzels, pasta, and chicken livers . . . ?** No, those aren't backstage snacks for the humans or animals, but low-tech props that are used during the special effects process. Don't look for them: Close your eyes and listen. Think about the sounds you hear

when the kids are morphing. "Creating the sound effects that go with the show is fun," Sue explains, exposing one of *Animorphs* deepest f/x secrets: You may never watch the show again without getting hungry. "That bone crunching sound you hear during the morphs? We do it by walking on a bag of pretzels! [Rold Gold, usually]. Or, sometimes for variation, we use a bag of penne pasta [uncooked, presumably]." As for the squishy sounds you hear in certain gross-out alert scenes? "Chicken livers being stirred in a bowl." [Bring on the onions!]

9. **Word play.** It's the job of the special effects department to come up with alien languages, and have the actors insert — or loop — that dialogue, plus all the <thought-speak> into the film after it's been shot. "For one episode, we actually had to invent the Andalite language," Sue says. "We decided that it might sound like English — backward. So we recorded the dialogue in English, and played it backward. Then, our actor came in and recited the backward dialogue."

10. **Much music.** Getting just the right "mood music" for each scene — tension, mystery, action, foreboding — falls under Sue's domain as well. The composer for the show, Norman Orenstein, watches each episode without any effects and goes to work creating original pieces.

Looking back on *Animorphs'* first season, Sue believes the special effects worked well — but she'd like to do even more amazing stuff for season two. "We haven't yet been able to morph animals as they're moving," she says. "That's something I'd like to try for the next round." That, and other awesome effects, are something to look forward to when *Animorphs* returns with fresh new episodes in the fall.

CHAPTER EIGHT

FACTS AT YOUR FINGERTIPS

See How the Real-life Actors Compare to Their Characters

TOTALLY TOBIAS

Nickname: Bird-boy

Family: Parents presumed dead; various aunts and uncles on both coasts

Closest Friends: Rachel; and Ax, Elfangor's younger brother

Hobbies: Reading, daydreaming, hanging at the mall, playing video games

Personality: Thoughtful, caring, instinctive, a dreamer

Morphs: Hawk . . . so far

Diet: As a hawk, he eats mice, rabbits, and other small animals

Morph Advice: "Take it from me, two hours, max!"

Quote: *"All I can think about is how great it feels . . . to have wings, I mean. You know, to be far above everything — to see things so clearly."*

CHRIS'S CORNER

Plays: Tobias
Full Name: Christopher Douglas Ralph
Birthday: May 13, 1977
Height: 5'10"
Hair: Brown
Eyes: Brown
Parents: Douglas, a junior high teacher; and Sandra, a homemaker
Brother: Gregory

Favorites

Music: All kinds — everything from the blues to the Beatles, from Oasis to Frank Sinatra. "Everything except Top 40," Chris says.

Singer: Bono from U2

Group: U2

Movies: *Edward Scissorhands* and *The Apostle*

Scary Movie: *Halloween, Part 4.* "This is the one where evil killer Michael Myers has been in a coma for fifteen years and he comes back to life while they're transferring him from one hospital to another."

Actors: "Johnny Depp — he's the guy I'd like to pattern my career after. He's an icon for me. Also Robert Duvall. He should have won the Oscar for *The Apostle.* Lately, I've started to appreciate Billy Bob Thornton, too. And you have to admire Leonardo DiCaprio — not just for *Titanic,* but before that, holding his own against Robert De Niro in *This Boy's Life.* That was amazing."

Material Possession: Chris wasn't the kind of kid

who cared a lot about material possessions — he still doesn't. "I never saved up to buy anything. I never wanted a big stereo or a car or anything. My needs are pretty simple."

His Advice to You: "Don't worry about things. Life exists after high school. I know it's difficult when you start to feel you're all by yourself, but it's not that big a deal. People who come out of it realize, now I can get on with things, and get into what I want to get into. Those are the people who have the mind-set to go after their goals.

"All I can say is find the thing you like to do, but don't obsess about it. Just enjoy doing it. If you like reading, and people make fun of you because you're alone in the library, reading a book, don't worry about it. That eventually is going to lead to something creative.

"And if acting is what you want, believe me, you're not going to feel like an outsider in that community. You're going to meet some weird people, and you're going to have a blast. It you have fun with it, take the initiative and go out and do some shows."

RACHEL ON THE REAL

Nicknames: Xena, Warrior Princess; Ms. Fashion
Family: Dad, Don, is a TV weatherman; Mom, Naomi, is a lawyer; they are divorced. Sara and Jordan are her younger sisters; Jake, an Animorph, is her cousin.
Best Bud: Cassie
Hobbies: Gymnastics and shopping

Personality: Smart, adventurous, headstrong
Best Trait: Courage
Morphs: Lion, housefly, cat, cockroach, butterfly
Morph Advice: "Keep your focus."
Quote: *"Wait a minute. Are you saying that some alien slug can crawl into our brains and take over our minds?"*

BROOKE'S NOOK

Plays: Rachel
Full Name: Brooke Candice Nevin
Birthday: December 22, 1982
Born and Raised: Toronto, Canada
Parents: mom, Nicky; and dad, Bob, a retired hockey player, who was on three teams: the NY Rangers, of which he was the captain, plus the Toronto Maple Leafs, and LA Kings.
Sister: Kaleigh Cassandra
Instrument Played: Piano
Fun Stuff to Do: Dancing and singing

Favorites

TV Shows: *Buffy the Vampire Slayer, Dawson's Creek, Candid Camera* ["My mom and I have a blast, she goes into convulsions when we watch *Candid Camera*"], *20/20,* and *Inside Edition.* "I like a lot of others, but I can't watch that much because I'm too busy."

Color: Red
Foods: Salads and Chinese food

Drink: Orange juice

Sports: Rollerblading, soccer, biking, volleyball, downhill skiing

After School Snack: Bagels

Board Game: Monopoly

You Might be Surprised to Know: Brooke has won numerous public speaking contests.

Collects: Brooke's childhood collections range from stickers to porcelain masks to coins.

Second Job: As if her plate wasn't already full, Brooke does a lot of baby-sitting because she loves little kids.

Biggest Fear When Starting a New School Year: "In high school I was afraid of everything! I was afraid about making friends, all the cliques, I was really afraid because I switched from the gifted program to French immersion program. I didn't know how [the kids in that program] would treat me, because they'd been together for six years, so I was afraid of not fitting in. But that didn't happen — I'm best friends with them now. It was silly."

Message to You: "Find something you're really interested in that you won't get tired of; research it, get into it."

JUST JAKE

Nicknames: Prince Jake, Fearless leader

Family: dad, Greg, a doctor; mom, Nicki, a writer; brother, Tom, human-Controller; cousin Rachel, Animorph

Best Bud: Marco
Crush: Cassie
Hobbies: Video games, sports
Personality: Strong, natural leader; cool under fire
Career Goals: Navy pilot and doctor
Morphs: Dog, cockroach, butterfly, lobster, tiger
Morph Advice: "Stay cool."
Quote: *"My name is Jake. That's all I can tell you. I can't tell you my last name, or where I live. Because the Controllers are everywhere. They could be anybody. They could be you."*

SHAWN'S STATS
Plays: Jake
Full Name: Shawn Robert Ashmore
Birthday: October 7, 1979
Born: Richmond, British Columbia
Grew Up In: Alberta and Ontario
Height: 5'11"
Hair: Brown
Eyes: Blue
Parents: Linda, homemaker; Rick, manufacturing company manager
Brother: Aaron, his twin. "Some people think there's no resemblance, and some people think we're exactly the same and can't tell us apart, so it's kind of weird."
Differences in Their Personalities: "Some people say Aaron's more aggressive than I am."
Pets: Jessica is the family's golden retriever, a birthday present Shawn got when he was nine. "We call her

Jessie, and what's really bizarre is that my dog on *Animorphs* is also a golden retriever named Jesse — except he's a boy."

Favorites

Music: "I listen to everything, from reggae to punk to hip-hop. Lately, I've been listening to a band called Bad Religion."

Movie: *Saving Private Ryan; As Good As It Gets*

Scary Movies: *Pet Cemetery; Candyman*

Food: "Spicy! Mexican, Thai, also sushi, which I never thought I'd like."

Drink: "Coke, or any kind of pop; juice, milk, water. I'm not too picky about what I drink."

Midnight Fridge Raid: Ham sandwich and a glass of milk

TV Show: "It used to be the *X-Files* and *Seinfeld*, now I'm not so sure. But I don't watch a lot of TV now."

TV Cartoon: *Ren and Stimpy.* "I used to love *Transformers* and *GI Joe.*"

Color: Blue. "I know this because I suddenly noticed that I have a lot of blue clothes. Otherwise, it's not something I think about."

Clothes: Far from a clotheshorse, Shawn does admit to impulse buys of jeans, shirts, and jackets mostly.

Place: "British Columbia, especially the coast. I love to sail, or go hang on the beach. I also love the mountains there for snowboarding."

For Fun: Music, whether it's listening to CDs or live; writing songs or playing guitar.

Lucky Charm: "A chain with a Libra charm, which is my astrological sign. My grandma gave it to me and I consider it a good luck charm. It's the only piece of jewelry I own."

CASSIE'S CORNER
Nicknames: Tree-hugger, Earth-mother [as Marco calls her]
Lives: On a farm
Family: dad, John, farm veterinarian; Mom, Aisha, zoo veterinarian
Best Bud: Rachel
Crush: Jake
Hobbies: Animals, animals, animals!
Personality: Perceptive, caring, compassionate, loyal, focused, levelheaded
Career Goal: Zoo veterinarian
Morphs: Horse, rabbit, skunk, cockroach, butterfly
Trademark: Best morpher of the group
Morph Advice: "Control the animal brain."
Quote: *"It was so awesome. I was a horse! I was powerful and fast. And I just wanted to run and run and feel the wind in my mane."*

NADIA'S NOTES
Plays: Cassie
Full Name: Nadia Leigh Nascimento
Birthdate: June 6, 1978
Birthplace: Vancouver, Canada

Lives Now: Toronto, Canada (when *Animorphs* films); and Vancouver
Height: 5'2"
Hair: Brown
Eyes: Brown
Parents: José and Beth Nascimento
Brother: Eric
Sister: Chantelle
School: Capilano College "I'm doing a transfer program from the University of British Columbia."
Major: "I started as a sociology major, but now I want to study business."
Instruments: Piano, violin, guitar, and harmonica
Favorites
  Actors: Tom Hanks, Denzel Washington, Harrison Ford, Jack Nicholson
  Actresses: Jodie Foster, Brooke Nevin
  TV Shows: *The Simpsons, Friends*
  Foods: "I don't care how you serve it — just give it to me! I especially like Greek food."
  Books: *Celestine Prophecy, The Land Where the Blues Began*
  Music: The blues
  Vacation Places: Sintra, Portugal; Cappadocia, Turkey
First Look at a Guy: "I love the way people walk — especially the way my boyfriend strides. And that whole smiling thing is a big plus."
What Keeps Her Interested: "Personality — when they're funny. Funny and smart — I'm stuck!"

Collections: "New Kids on the Block stuff, including trading cards, comic books, pretty much anything!"
Dream Trip: "I have to go to Brazil. I have family there."
Self-Description: "I'm very extroverted. I love a lot and I'm caring."

MEET MARCO

Family: dad, Jeremy, engineer/night maintenance; mom, Laura, presumed dead
Best Bud: Jake
Hobbies: Anything video, thrill rides, hanging with Jake, giving Rachel a hard time
Personality: Cute, witty, smart, sarcastic
Favorite Word: "Insane"
Best Trait: Great sense of humor
Trademark: Came up with the name, Animorphs
Morphs: Python, rat, cockroach, butterfly
Morph Advice: "Kids, don't try this at home!"
Quote: *"Believe it or not, I still have an algebra exam tomorrow, even if aliens are taking over the world."*

BASIC BORIS

Plays: Marco
Full Name: Boris Alberto Cabrera (he was named after his grandfather)
Birthday: December 16, 1980
Birthplace: Inglewood, California
Grew Up In: Pacoima, CA

Lives Now: In Toronto, for *Animorphs;* otherwise, it's home to California
Height: 5'6"
Hair: Black
Eyes: Brown
Parents: George Arturo and Eugenia Mercedes Cabrera
Brother: Arturo
Pets: Marco's beloved German shepherd, Wolfie, recently passed away
Car: A cherry-red '66 Mustang, which Boris is restoring
Buff Boy: He's into weight lifting. Boris has an entire setup in the backyard of his parents' house
Sports: Karate and wrestling
First Professional Job: A Coke commercial
Favorites
   Actors: Al Pacino, Robert De Niro
   Film: *Scarface*
   TV Show: *The Larry Sanders Show* (recently canceled)
   Singer: Sade
   Food: Ribs
   Book: *All Summer and a Day* by Ray Bradbury
   Color: Turquoise
   Place: The highest point of Mulholland Drive in LA. "You can see the whole city of LA on one side, and the entire San Fernando Valley on the other from there. That's my favorite."
   Board Game: Monopoly

First Look at a Girl: "It's important to me for a girl to be fit, because I work out. It's a priority."

What Keeps Him Interested: "Mental level, definitely. We have to be able to have an intelligent conversation."

Collections: Baseball cards and comic books

Dream Trip: "I'd like to go to Egypt and see the pyramids."

Self-Description: "I'm a happy person."

INFORMATION STATION

REACH OUT AND TOUCH

You can reach the stars of *Animorphs* in a variety of ways.

Snail Mail: Address your letter to the Ani-star of your choice, and send it either to: *Animorphs*, Nickelodeon, 1515 Broadway, New York, NY 10036. Or: *Animorphs,* Scholastic Productions, 524 Broadway, New York, NY 10012. All letters sent to those addresses will be forwarded to the actor you chose.

The *official* Animorphs website, **www.scholastic.-com/animorphs,** provides fans with a truly interactive Animorphs experience. Kids can preview upcoming episodes, download cast photos and get the scoop on the stars and storylines with exclusive behind-the-scenes information. The millions of readers of the book series can look forward to a preview of the next highly anticipated release, email Animorphs author K.A. Applegate, and learn more about book cover artist David Mattingly. Additionally, the site enables visitors to electronically send Animorphs postcards to their friends, and win official merchandise related to the book and TV series by participating in online games and contests.

Animorphs Stuff

The Ani-"merch" invasion has begun — and it's spreading as fast as the popularity of the books, TV show, and stars. You can now wear, play, take to school, and even *eat* official *Animorphs*-related stuff.

Aside from the requisite T-shirts, devoted fans will find everything from backpacks to boxers, bookcovers, and beach towels, available at stores and boutiques all over the USA. Tiger Electronics has handheld games and Hasbro's got a full line, including board games, video games, and puzzles, plus ultra-cool "triple morph" collectible figurines, from the Transformers collection.

And there's a VIDEO series, too! Coming soon, from Scholastic Productions and Columbia Tri Star Home Video, a collection of full-length videos compiled of the best episodes from season one of the show. The video launch is spring '99 and the videos will have never-been-seen-before footage!

Book It!

Cool as the TV series is, *Animorphs* is first and foremost the best-selling book series in North America — there are over 15 million books out there already, with lots more to come.

Alien Facts: A Glossary of Terms

Andalite

Possessing the unique power to morph, the Andalites, an alien race, are on a quest to save the galaxy from Yeerk takeover. With the combined appearance of a horse, deer, human, and scorpion, the Andalites have long, powerful tails with a scythe-like blade at the end. Their four legs end in hooves and their thin arms in many-fingered hands. Without a mouth, the Andalite's triangular face is flat, with three vertical slits for a nose and two large, green, almond-shaped eyes. From atop the head rise two "stalk eyes" that can move independently of the main eyes in any direction. Andalite fur, usually blue, can also range from brown to pale green to lavender.

Ax (short for Aximili-Esgarrouth-Isthill)

An heroic two-year-old Andalite (fourteen, in Earth years), Ax is the Animorphs' greatest alien ally. His brother, Prince Elfangor, was the Andalite who entrusted the Animorphs with the ability to morph into any animal they touch. Ax looks like the other Andalites and shares their remarkable powers of morphing, speed, and strength. In his human morph, Ax is a mix of DNA borrowed from Jake, Rachel, Cassie, and Marco and loves to use his mouth to make fascinating human sounds and to taste every possible kind of delicious human food.

Controller

When a Yeerk has enslaved a host, the host becomes a Controller. Controllers, in turn, try to acquire new hosts — preferably people in authority, and children, who are rarely suspect. They gain voluntary entry into the minds of their hosts with bribes of money and power, cures for diseases, revenge against enemies, help with crises, and the powerful urge to "belong." Involuntary means are used only when absolutely necessary. Controllers may also be referred to in the hyphenated form, for example, a "human-Controller," for an enslaved human.

Hork-Bajir

A horrifying alien that stands seven feet tall, with a snakelike head, powerful long arms, and bent-back legs like a dinosaur. Sharp-horned blades grow from its head, elbows, forearms, and knees. Its fingers end in needle-sharp nails and its gargantuan feet are like ripping claws. Ironically, the Hork-Bajir is by nature gentle, kind, and peaceful; its arsenal of blades is actually an evolutionary adaptation for stripping off tree bark, its basic food.

Kandrona Rays

The subatomic particles produced by the Yeerks' home sun, upon which the Yeerks are dependent.

When traveling the galaxy, the Yeerks may obtain these particles from artificial Kandrona rays, or Yeerk pools. A Yeerk pool exists on the Yeerk mother ship and others may be hidden someplace on Earth.

Thought-speak

Thought-speak is the natural language of the Andalite race. A form of mental telepathy, thought-speak can also be used to transmit pictures, ideas, and concepts. Thought-speak is also used by the Animorphs when they are morphed.

Yeerk

Once a fairly harmless parasite confined to a single planet, the Yeerk is now the scourge of the entire galaxy. A gray-green slug about six to seven inches long, a Yeerk infests the brain of its prey via an ear canal and commands control of its victim's free will. The slimy predator has taken over any number of species throughout its galactic dominion, but, currently, maintains an insatiable craving for humans.

Yeerk Pool

Every three days, Yeerks must return to a Yeerk pool, consisting of artificial Kandrona rays or subatomic particles produced by the Yeerks' home sun. Here, they drain out of their host's ear and soak up vital nutrients. A Controller who fails to report to the Yeerk pool after three days begins to lose control of his host and the Yeerk dies.

Visser Three

A powerful Yeerk general, Visser Three reports to the supreme Yeerk ruling body. Vissers are numbered according to power and seniority, and Visser Three holds a very high rank in the Yeerk chain of command. His current responsibility is Earth, which puts him and his many warriors in direct and constant battle against the Animorphs. Visser Three believes the Animorphs are escaped Andalites because of their ability to morph. Visser Three is the only Andalite-Controller, the first Yeerk ever to infest an Andalite body and gain its powerful morphing capabilities. In fact, Visser Three had been all over the universe acquiring the genetic patterns of monsters that have never been seen on Earth. While on Earth, Visser Three poses as Victor Trent, a powerful and wealthy businessman.